More Readers Theatre for Middle School Boys

Recent Titles in Teacher Ideas Press
Readers Theatre Series

Wings of Fancy: Using Readers Theatre to Study Fantasy Genre
Joan Garner

Nonfiction Readers Theatre for Beginning Readers
Anthony D. Fredericks

Mother Goose Readers Theatre for Beginning Readers
Anthony D. Fredericks

MORE Frantic Frogs and Other Frankly Fractured Folktales for Readers Theatre
Anthony D. Fredericks

Songs and Rhymes Readers Theatre for Beginning Readers
Anthony D. Fredericks

Readers Theatre for Middle School Boys: Investigating the Strange and Mysterious
Ann N. Black

African Legends, Myths, and Folktales for Readers Theatre
Anthony D. Fredericks

Against All Odds: Readers Theatre for Grades 3-8
Suzanne I. Barchers and Michael Ruscoe

Readers Theatre for African American History
Jeff Sanders and Nancy I. Sanders

Building Fluency with Readers Theatre: Motivational Strategies, Successful Lessons, and Dynamic
Scripts to Develop Fluency, Comprehension, Writing, and Vocabulary
Anthony D. Fredericks

American Folklore, Legends, and Tall Tales for Readers Theatre
Anthony D. Fredericks

Multi-Grade Readers Theatre: Picture Book Authors and Illustrators
Suzanne I. Barchers and Charla R. Pfeffinger

More Readers Theatre for Middle School Boys

Adventures with Mythical Creatures

Ann N. Black

Illustrated by Cody Rust

Readers Theatre

A Teacher Ideas Press Book

Libraries Unlimited

An Imprint of ABC-CLIO, LLC

A B C 🌊 C L I O

Santa Barbara, California • Denver, Colorado • Oxford, England

Library of Congress Cataloging-in-Publication Data

Black, Ann N.
  More readers theatre for middle school boys : adventures with mythical creatures / Ann N. Black.
      p. cm. — (Readers theatre series)
  Includes bibliographical references and index.
    ISBN 978-1-59158-757-6 (pbk : alk. paper) 1. Animals, Mythical—Juvenile drama. 2. Children's plays, American. 3. Readers' theater. 4. Drama in education. 5. Mythology—Study and teaching (Secondary)—Activity programs. I. Title.
  PS3602.L245M67 2009
  812'.6—dc22   2009011978

13   12   11   10   9   1   2   3   4   5

This book is also available on the World Wide Web as an eBook.
Visit www.abc-clio.com for details.

ABC-CLIO, LLC
130 Cremona Drive, P.O. Box 1911
Santa Barbara, California 93116-1911

This book is printed on acid-free paper ∞™
Manufactured in the United States of America

Contents

Acknowledgments

I am again indebted to The British Museum, the Tutt Library of Colorado College, and the Pikes Peak Library District for their resources and knowledgeable staff members, who were invaluable in the research for this book. In addition, I appreciate the astute editing by Sharon DeJohn, which has added immeasurably to clarifying several difficult subjects. Cody Rust's inventive illustrations have been a joy to include. I am deeply grateful for the warm encouragement of Peter Maxfield; for the love and faith of sons Bob, Bill, and Casey; and as always, for the steady guidance and support of Hugh Rae in Scotland. Above all, this effort would be meaningless without the affection, vitality, and wise criticisms of my friends and colleagues, the Calabashers—Marty Banks, Linda Duval, Maria Faulconer, Toni Knapp, and Susan Rust.

Introduction

Why on earth would we want to take a group of middle school boys on adventures into mythical worlds? We will be leading them into strange, foreign lands, skirting the globe. When we start dipping way back in time, we have to bridge great gaps of no-knowledge. What will they actually learn/love from these adventures?

Perhaps they will acquire that "respectful tone toward cultures, customs, and beliefs" that Marge Freeburn and her teaching colleagues consider essential for young readers.[1] On the other hand, the brief essay by a thirteen-year-old boy in a 2008 issue of *Publishers Weekly* calls for "vampires and other supernatural creatures," as he believes young readers "have a much higher tolerance for horror and action than most adults."[2] Indeed, according to a recent survey reported in *The Washington Post*: "The most-read book among seventh-and eighth-graders was *The Outsiders*, a story of rival gangs in Tucson."[3] Adventuring into the myths with readers theatre, we may not be too surprised to find that learn/love go hand in hand.

Myths, unlike legends, are not necessarily based on historical fact. They are stories spun from the oral traditions of early peoples. The truths that sustain them, however, reveal moral and spiritual values that underlie the historical facts recorded later in time.

For example, traveling to Africa to meet the god Eshu, we find a myth that illustrates the mistrust and misunderstanding that can occur between long-standing friends. Or when we venture into the early times of present-day Iraq to follow the tortured road of Gilgamesh, we participate in his journey as he forgoes his overweening pride and discovers the true meaning in his life. Confronting the monster gorgon, Medusa, we come face to face with power that must be defeated in one swift, gory blow by the determined hero, Perseus.

Stories from ancient civilizations set us up for truly mythical powers. We are seeking heroes—people who rise to greatness because of a cause greater than themselves. True, some of the heroes are part god, but we accept that—just as we accept the transformation of Superman. Something incredible happens, but the world is saved—for the time being.

Heroes such as Cuchulain, Siegfried, and Hercules transcend mere human abilities. Yet the struggles they endure, and the obstacles they must overcome, are all too human. Actions of the Irish hero Cuchulain bespeak pride, valor, and patriotism. The Nordic hero, Siegfried, confronts avarice and bullying from a deadly dragon and tricky gnomes. The Greek Hercules, who seems to have moved from human to god, must undertake incredible Labors to mitigate the horrors he has caused—actions others made him perform.

Multiple physical characteristics emphasize the elusive recognition that things are not always what they seem. In the Pueblo Indian myth, for example, evil has many faces. One such personification occurs in the Norse stories about Loki, the famous Trickster. When he appears, bad things happen to good people. As we trace the avatars of Vishnu, the Hindu god, we begin to see the broad ramifications of evil in the world and the attempts of mythical creatures to squelch them.

Often these larger-than-life adventures with evil come with a lot of blood and guts: Perseus decapitates Medusa; Hercules chokes the furious three-headed dog at the gates of Hades; Siegfried tastes the dragon's blood; and the Chinook god, Thunderer, drowns the Giant who threatens to eat five young brothers.

But what good is the potential excitement and historic value of these myths, if middle school boys are reluctant to pick up a book and read about them? Reading silently, to one's self, has definite advantages—benefits we would like to see all students appreciate. But does this happen? Unfortunately, statistics and anecdotal evidence tell us otherwise. Maybe the book assigned for silent reading is too long? Or the words are too difficult? Perhaps the students can't figure out the pronunciation?

Reading aloud, as a team effort, can do away with some of that reading reluctance. Foreign names and places can come alive with imaginative reading aloud. So *Eshu* may sound like a sneeze—okay! *Cuchulain* looks formidable—but it has only three syllables (*Ku-ku-linn'*). So does Chicago (*Sheh-kah'-go*).

In addition to mastering unusual pronunciations, punctuation takes on a whole new value with oral reading. Meaning is enhanced or destroyed with the dash, those commas, and semicolons. The period really becomes the *full stop*, as they call it in England. Reading aloud, students must convey the meaning and emotion to an audience, not just to themselves. They have a new obligation with reading; evaluating the punctuation is just one tool for them.

When boys become part of a *reading team,* everyone is equally important—everyone contributes; everyone benefits. Everyone depends on everyone else. Reading a story aloud in a group effort shifts personal fears and aggrandizement to the presentation of something larger—the literature at hand. This is when readers theatre can be a godsend.

WHAT, EXACTLY, IS READERS THEATRE?

First of all, readers theatre is not *theatre* in the usual sense. It does not need a stage or special lighting, costumes, or makeup. Readers theatre needs only a space large enough to accommodate fifteen students without crowding. Such a stage space could be in the school auditorium, the cafeteria, or simply in the classroom.

Readers theatre does not rely on actors who move around and somehow resemble dramatic characters. It needs, wants, and must have, oral readers, sensitive and informed, to present the emotional and intellectual content of words—the be-all and end-all in a readers theatre performance. Readers assume the responsibility for interpreting the imagination of storytellers who have given us their words to share.

When myths are on the program, the readers are re-creating the oral traditions of early storytellers. They're not sitting around a campfire to tell the stories, but they are invoking some of the magic that surrounded the storytellers and fascinated their listeners.

Today, listeners—the audience and classmates—do not attend a readers theatre performance looking for education. They want to be entertained. But both education and entertainment can come about when they are engaged with the basic drama of stories presented by a dedicated group of oral readers.

The mention of *drama* inevitably returns us to the distinctions between conventional theatre and readers theatre. Except for purely improvisational theatre, both styles of theatre begin with written scripts. Instructions and background information for the director of these scripts may include a list of the cast, the required technical effects, and suggestions for the presentation of these components. Then the gulf widens.

Scripts for conventional theatre must be memorized. Not so for readers theatre. Scripts must be well read and well interpreted, but not memorized—a boon for the inexperienced! The casting for conventional dramatic productions is often extremely restrictive, because physical abilities and appearances must be taken into consideration. These are not major concerns in readers theatre. Voice qualities might influence a casting choice, but height, weight, and ethnicity are not problems.

Technical requirements for conventional theatre can range from the extreme simplicity of *Our Town's* staging to the high-tech world of *Miss Saigon*, in which helicopters appear to land on stage. Readers theatre, on the other hand, needs only general lighting, chairs or stools, and perhaps reading stands.

Positions on the space/stage should reflect the relative importance of the characters. Traditional use of the stage also corresponds to the needs of readers theatre. Placement is one factor. Height is another. Visibility is primary; we don't want any reader performing directly in front of another.

To begin with, each stage has six main areas. With the cast facing the audience, the following plan shows the relative importance of the stage areas for readers theatre, X1 being the strongest position.

Up right X4	Up center X5	Up left X6
Down right X2	Down center X1	Down left X3

Each of the scripts in this book follows this pattern as much as possible, allowing for the inevitable variations in the height of the cast members. In general, the most important characters (readers) stand in the front row, the less important in the back. The readers in the front row should be spaced so they do not block the readers in the row behind.

What about costumes? In a conventional theatre production, costumes may range from a simple peasant's outfit to lavish royal robes and gowns. Cast members in a readers theatre production do not try to visually impersonate the characters in the story, nor do they try to emulate the characters, except vocally and emotionally.

The cast will want to make a good impression on their audience, so a certain uniformity of clothes might be encouraged—maybe all in jeans with black or white T-shirts. Individual flamboyant accessories (chains, medals, slogans, etc.), of course, are discouraged. These readers want to present a sensitive oral interpretation of the script, using no more than their physical attitudes, their voices, their eyes, and perhaps their hands.

This is a tall order. What can we expect from such participation?

Students who participate in readers theatre grow, for "[t]o understand the thoughts of another mind, fixed in print, to read beyond one's own experience means to identify with that mind, to learn the physical satisfactions of frustrations behind it, and to understand the ideas and emotions that have evolved from it."[4]

Furthermore, imagination kicks in as the "mind's eye" offers our middle school boys a new appreciation for silent, personal reading. They may be prompted to write their own myths. They may be inspired to illustrate the mythical heroes and creatures they've just met. By engaging in readers theatre, teachers and students alike will find that literacy and enjoyment can go hand in hand.

A PRÉCIS OF THE READERS THEATRE SCRIPTS

The scripts in this book have been written for middle school boys who are ready for adventures with mythical creatures, both the mysterious and the enigmatic.

"Eshu the Trickster" is based on the African tale of a sly god, Eshu, known as the Trickster. Eshu's strange actions first threaten, then strengthen, the friendship of two Nigerian farmers.

"Passing the Torch," rooted in the lore of the Chinook Indians, explores the transfer of power and the inherited values of good and evil.

"Captured!" is drawn from the oral storytelling of the Pueblo Indians and dramatizes a bizarre adventure that occurs when innocence, ignorance, and evil collide.

"The Quest of Gilgamesh," based on an epic poem of Babylonian times, follows the drastic events that torment the life of the ancient king, Gilgamesh.

"Hercules and the Watchdog of Hades" traces the legendary Labors of the hero, Hercules, as he battles to atone for his horrible misdeeds.

"Searching for Snakes" is a retelling of the journey of Perseus, who finds the Gorgon Medusa—she with a nest of snakes for hair and eyes that turn men to stone—and beheads her.

"Avatar Adventures with Vishnu" hovers over the realistic, but mythical exploits of Vishnu, the venerable god of India who tries to save all humanity from evil.

"An Ancient Irish Hero, Cuchulain" is based on early Irish tales of a warrior king, Cuchulain, who is revered even today for his legendary prowess and bravery.

"The Taste of Dragon's Blood" dips into the complex folklore that surrounds the Scandinavian/Germanic hero, Siegfried; his nemeses, the Niebelungs; and a sinister dragon out to kill.

"Loki—Evil Tricks in Asgard" concentrates on the chaotic actions of the Norse Trickster Loki and shows how repercussions from other gods could be swift and deadly.

NOTES

1. Marge Freeburn, "Recent Trends in Literature about the Middle East for Teens and Young Adults: Afghanistan, Iraq, and Pakistan," *Statement* (Summer 2008): 19.

2. Max Leone, "read this b4 u publish," *Publishers Weekly* (November 10, 2008): 54.

3. Jay Matthews, "What Do Children Read? Hint: Harry Potter's Not No.1," *Washington Post,* May 5, 2008, A01. Available at www.washingtonpost.com/dyn/content/article/2008/05/04AR2008050401785.html (accessed August 10, 2008).

4. Ann N. Black, "A Literary Commune" (master's thesis, University of North Texas, 1974), 36.

Myths from Around the World: Africa

Eshu the Trickster

INTRODUCTION

The classic Trickster of mythology can appear in various and surprising guises, but his character is undeniable and unforgiving. He plays the rogue, the cheat, the joker, the spoiler. In fact, with his mercurial personality he might be seen as the original, consummate knave in storytelling. The African god Eshu, the Trickster who practices this chicanery, appears in several myths of the Yoruba people, who now reside in Benin and southwestern Nigeria.

Eshu (or Edshu) is a god or spirit, an *orisha*, and as such has the freedom and the wherewithal to play tricks among the people on Earth. With his cunning nature and capricious actions, he stirs up human troubles and, consequently, human fears.

At the same time, the god Eshu has a dark history that might provoke his behavior and influence his personality. After he offended the High God with one of his nefarious schemes, Eshu was relegated to being the messenger of the gods. Still, as a bona fide deity, Eshu is honored with sacrifices, statuary, and shrines, which are frequently placed at crossroads and in the marketplace.

Although European efforts at colonization brought about many changes to the Yoruba, the arts and crafts of the people have continued to flourish, especially the woodcarvings of splendid masks and figures. Fine pottery, weaving, and metal work often come together to personify various rituals and beliefs. Given the richness of this civilization, it is no wonder that the complexities of Eshu, the Trickster, have inspired so many to translate his unique qualities into enduring works of art.

PRODUCTION NOTES

Need we mention that homemade African masks and almost any chocolate bar will provide valuable additions to this production? They're not necessary, of course, but such touches are bound to add to the fun. (Hot chocolate would be good, too!)

The script for "Eshu the Trickster" calls for a cast of approximately fourteen boys. To adjust this number, the lines of some characters can be combined (e.g., Chieftains 1 and 2), and the Tribal Chorus can be doubled or even cut in half. Theoretically, fifteen scripts will be needed, which includes one for the teacher.

Travelers 1 and 2 are the guides on this journey.

The Vendor of cocoa provides some local color and sound. He has two small cloth or leather bags. One holds "cocoa pods," or a reasonable facsimile. The other has coins.

The Tribal Chorus provides enthusiasm and comments vis-à-vis the audience.

Griot is the storyteller, or mythmaker. He is essentially our narrator.

Eshu, of course, is the rogue god. He has to have fun with his missions!

Farmers 1 and 2 are earnest friends who also blow up in earnest.

Chieftains 1 and 2 are the peacekeepers, firm but apt to be confused.

P.S. Spellings in mythology can vary considerably, but whether we use Edshu or Eshu, the name still sounds like a sneeze!

Eshu the Trickster

Eshu the Trickster

From African Myths

		Tribal Chorus			
		X X X X			
	Vendor		Shopkeeper	Chieftains 1, 2	
	X		X	X X	
Eshu	Griot	Farmer 1	Farmer 2	Travelers 1, 2	
X	X	X	X	X X	

TRAVELER 1: I have no idea where we are, but the smell is fantastic. It's chocolate!

TRAVELER 2: Aren't you following the map? We're in the heart of Africa now!

TRAVELER 1: Oh, sure, and chocolate pots are cooking around every palm tree.

TRAVELER 2: Not palm trees—*cocoa* trees. We're in Nigeria, and what an adventure this will be! Take a look at those masks—and keep on grinning.

VENDOR: (*Shakes his bag of nuts*) Fresh cocoa pods! You buy? Very nice—fresh.

TRAVELER 1: Over here, man. And I'm not even going to ask if they're organic. Masks or no masks, just pass the chocolate! Okay?

TRIBAL CHORUS: Hot chocolate! Hot chocolate!

TRAVELER 1: Now—I *will* ask this: Why all the chocolate in Nigeria?

TRAVELER 2: So glad you asked. Nigeria produces mountains of cocoa every year—a great background for our mythic adventure, right? So listen up for the Trickster god from Africa, Eshu. (*Es'-shoo*)

TRAVELER 1: Eshu? (*Laughs*) Sounds like a sneeze! Eshu!

TRIBAL CHORUS: Eshu! Eshu!

TRAVELER 2: Be serious! This god plays tricks on people and causes them trouble.

TRAVELER 1: A practical joker? That's pretty weird for a god—but I'm ready.

VENDOR: (*Shakes his bag of coins, too*) You gonna pay for chocolate? Then you gonna hear storyteller. The griot—he is gonna tell funny myth, then bad myth. You wanna buy the chocolate? (*gree-o'*)

TRAVELER 2: Okay, we'll pay. You fetch the griot. We'll wait.

TRIBAL CHORUS: (*Softly*) Shush. (*Pause, then louder*) Shush. Griot.

GRIOT: Welcome. Welcome. You sit—the night is cold. Draw near the fire.

TRAVELER 1: (*In a loud whisper*) Do you think it's all right if I bring along my hot chocolate? This may be a long night.

TRAVELER 2: (*In a loud whisper*) Hush! Sit down!

GRIOT: Good. Chocolate is good medicine—but we've got some bad history with Eshu. He's a very tricky god, you know. In two stories, you will see. Eshu hoodwinks two wives and then two farmers—with hats.

TRIBAL CHORUS: Tell. Tell!

GRIOT: The stories come from long, long ago—back when our people first came to this land.

TRAVELER 2: The Yorubas. I know that!

GRIOT: Come from the Sahara—very big. Much sand and wind now. Yoruba people walk many days, some all the way to the big waters—the ocean.

TRAVELER 1: Well, the ocean's not too far away, and it's pretty green around here.

GRIOT: Very good for farmers. Some grow very rich—even own two wives.

TRAVELER 1: I call that double trouble.

TRIBAL CHORUS: Shush!

GRIOT: No trouble—until our god Eshu *makes* trouble.

TRIBAL CHORUS: Look out! Look out! Eshu!

GRIOT: Eshu is most powerful spirit—an orisha—a *Trickster* god. Now, trouble begins for one rich man who had two wives. (*o-ree'-shah*)

TRIBAL CHORUS: Look out! Eshu!

GRIOT: Trouble began when number-one wife visited the village shopkeeper.

SHOPKEEPER: Good morning, madam. How can I help you?

ESHU: Step aside, merchant. I believe this lovely lady might be interested in a special hat for her husband. (*Pause*) Allow me, Madam, to show you this headdress bound in gold and pearls. Surely, this hat is fit for a king.

GRIOT: Well, Eshu overwhelmed the lady with that hat. She knew her husband would love it—and then maybe love *her* even more. Well, she was right on both counts.

TRAVELER 1: Uh-oh. Trouble's brewing! How did the man's *second* wife take that?

GRIOT: Went just a little bit jealous. The next day, as you can imagine, *she* appeared at the merchant's shop. Again, it was Eshu who greeted her.

ESHU: Ah, Madam, you of such excellent taste, would you like a splendid hat for your husband? Perhaps you'd like this shiny, silver cotton one, all laced with brilliant shells.

SHOPKEEPER: She knew her husband would like it better than the headdress the other wife had bought. So she bought it. Now, that made the *first* wife furious. She came right back to my shop.

ESHU: Of course! She bought another, an even fancier hat for her husband—this one I'd had embroidered in rich, feather threads of purple and gold.

TRAVELER 1: Now what? It's the second wife—jealous again, correct?

GRIOT: Exactly. Day after day, and one by one, the two wives went to the village to buy another even more splendid hat for their husband.

TRAVELER 2: How does this competition end?

GRIOT: In disaster. Eshu stopped bringing hats. He disappeared. The wives became angry and began to quarrel with each other. Their once happy home became a hive of jealousy.

TRAVELER 1: I sense a moral here.

TRAVELER 2: For sure, Eshu made them think: What *really* made them happy?

TRAVELER 1: Certainly not the hats!

SHOPKEEPER: No—not *those* hats. Now I sell plain, straw hats without any decoration, hats our farmers wear to keep off the sun.

TRAVELER 1: Those farmers again!

GRIOT: Yes, then and now and always—farmers growing rubber trees and cotton and fields of golden yams.

TRAVELER 1: Yams? Like sweet potatoes?

TRIBAL CHORUS: (*Definitely*) Yes, yams!

TRAVELER 1: Oh, yams are okay—I suppose—but what happened to the chocolate?

VENDOR: (*Shakes his bag of pods as he sings out his wares*) Cocoa pods! Cocoa!

TRAVELER 2: Cocoa man—later! Another story now. Griot—more Trickster?

GRIOT: Okay. Long ago, two men and their families also came to this land from the Sahara. The two men were good friends. They did everything together, and in the same way. They farmed the same way, they dressed the same way, and they thought the same about everything.

TRAVELER 1: Some people are like that—weird!

GRIOT: Well, these men saw the land was good, so they decided to settle here, and they staked out their fields right across the road from each other.

TRAVELER 1: Ah, for planting cocoa trees, right?

GRIOT: Yes, yes—but mainly for planting cotton and those yams.

TRIBAL CHORUS: Ummm. Yams!

FARMER 1: The gods have been kind to us, friend—even to me. But my fields *never* look as good as yours.

FARMER 2: Nonsense, neighbor. Look at those straight, even rows of new plants. I don't know *how* you do it.

FARMER 1: You flatter me, friend. It was you that gave me those healthy shoots. I am indebted to you!

FARMER 2: Don't mention it, brother. Remember that wild boar you saw digging in my fields?

FARMER 1: How could I forget him! I swear by the gods his snout was two feet long, and his hooves dug into the dirt like wild lions.

FARMER 2: Well, it was *you* who trapped that beast! You saved my crop that year! I can never repay you.

FARMER 1: Nonsense. That's what friends are for, right?

GRIOT: Good friends, *until* the Trickster god Eshu came to earth and interfered.

ESHU: Oh, oh! I'm looking down there, and I think people are just too calm. They're too satisfied—too happy. (*Pause*) Perhaps I can stir things up a bit. (*Pause*) Yes, that's an excellent idea! (*Pause*) Now, look at those two happy men. They walked right by my shrine this morning. No palm oil to anoint my shrine for three days! We'll see about that!

TRIBAL CHORUS: Look out! Eshu!

GRIOT: The very next morning, a strange man came strolling down the country road past the fields of our two farmers. The friends stopped digging in their fields to watch the man. They could tell he was a stranger—he was wearing an unusual hat.

TRAVELER 2: The plot thickens—more hats!

TRAVELER 1: Hush. Don't interrupt.

GRIOT: That evening, after the two farmers had finished their chores, they sat down to discuss the stranger over a cup of hot chocolate.

TRIBAL CHORUS: Yummmmm!

FARMER 1: Did you see that stranger walk down our road this morning?

FARMER 2: Sure did. Couldn't miss him. He had on a red hat.

FARMER 1: Red? No, friend. The hat was white.

FARMER 2: White? I beg your pardon, friend. I saw this man *and* his red hat with my own two eyes.

FARMER 1: Are we talking about the same man? He walked down the road right past me. I could see very clearly that his hat was white.

FARMER 2: No, brother! I saw this very same man, but he had on a *red* hat. I looked closely—at him and at his hat.

FARMER 1: (*Tensely*) Listen! I *know* what I saw—a man with a white hat walking up the road.

FARMER 2: Are you blind? (*Slowly, definitely*) The man who walked down the road past our fields was wearing a *very red* hat!

FARMER 1: (*Becoming angry*) I'm not blind! I know what I saw. But you—you must be drunk! What did you put in that hot chocolate?

FARMER 2: Nothing! If you don't want to believe *me* (*Pause*), maybe my knife will convince you. (*Angrily*) The hat was *red* not *white*!

FARMER 1: (*Defiantly*) A knife, eh? (*Laughs*) I have one of those, and it's sharp, too!

GRIOT: The men kicked back their wooden stools and raised their weapons. Their eyes flashed like wild men. Their jaws clenched in anger.

FARMER 2: You think you're better than I am—is that right? You think you know it all. Well, let me tell you right now, you're wrong! I know what I saw, and you're a liar!

FARMER 1: Liar? You see this knife? If you don't believe what I say, maybe this blade will help you remember—the hat the man wore was white!

FARMER 2: That does it! I've had enough of you!

GRIOT: Their hot chocolate forgotten—their families, their friendship forgotten—the two men bent down, ready to spring at their new enemy.

CHIEFTAIN 1: Stop! Stop, I say. Stop this instant! Drop those knives!

10

FARMER 1:   Go away! This is no concern of yours!

CHIEFTAIN 1:   You're wrong. It *is* my concern. I am here to keep the peace. You two men are destroying it for everyone!

CHIEFTAIN 2:   Drop the knives! The chieftain is right. You have broken the peace.

CHIEFTAIN 1:   So. We meet tomorrow, sunrise, at the council hut. You *will be there.*

GRIOT: The village elders stood watching and waiting. Slowly, the knives came down. The fierce, hot breathing of the two angry men faded away.

FARMER 1:   (*Tough and bitter*) Sunrise—tomorrow.

FARMER 2:   (*Angry*) Good. I'll be there to speak the truth for all to see!

CHIEFTAIN 2:   Yes, yes—the truth. Well, we'll see. Tomorrow at sunrise.

GRIOT: The fight was over, at least for a while. Perhaps a sunrise meeting at the council hut would be able to resolve this argument. Certainly each man was prepared to tell the elders what *he* thought was the truth.

TRIBAL CHORUS: (*Loud whisper*) Eshu. Remember Eshu.

CHIEFTAIN 2:   So, the sun burns with the dawn, and we are together. We must read the signs of the oracle. The palm nuts have been cast. They will speak to us. Ah! So! The gods accept your long-delayed sacrifice. You may begin.

GRIOT: The story came tumbling out. The chieftains and the elders were baffled. The story of the hat—or hats—did not make sense to them.

CHIEFTAIN 1:   Council agrees on one thing. Some sort of trick has taken place.

11

CHIEFTAIN 2: Trick? By heaven! We must look to the orisha—to the god Eshu.

TRIBAL CHORUS: (*Softly*) Aaaahhhh. Eshu!

CHIEFTAIN 2: He must be summoned.

CHIEFTAIN 1: Yes! Eshu! (*Louder*) Eshu!

ESHU: (*Laughs*) You called? (*Laughs*) I'm at your service!

CHIEFTAIN 1: Honored god Eshu, please, we welcome you to the Yoruba Council. We have great need of your wisdom.

CHIEFTAIN 2: Tell us, please, god Eshu, what has happened to these two fine farmers. They have long been friends, but they are friends no more.

FARMER 2: That's because *he's* blind! I *know* what I saw! A stranger came walking down our road wearing a red hat. Correct?

FARMER 1: He's drunk! I'm telling the truth, god Eshu! His hat was white!

GRIOT: Then our Trickster god began to laugh—for *he* was the stranger.

ESHU: Of course, you're both right! I painted one side of my hat red and the other side white. Each of you could see only *one* side—only *one* color.

CHIEFTAIN 1: But these men say you walked up the road and down.

CHIEFTAIN 2: Yes, but when you turned around, each still saw either red or white.

ESHU: (*Laughs*) When I turned around, I turned my hat, too. *You* still saw the red side, and *you* still saw the white.

GRIOT: Everyone was stunned. The farmers couldn't believe what Eshu was telling them. Yet after a moment, they saw they'd been fooled.

TRAVELER 1: Me, too! What a sneaky trick! The two friends are enemies now.

GRIOT: Maybe. Maybe stronger friends. The trick taught them to look beyond the obvious and to trust each other's views, even if they're different.

TRAVELER 2: So what did the two farmers do? Just go home?

GRIOT: Yes—but first, they had to smile, at everyone and at each other. Then they shook hands and went to their own fields and their own homes.

TRAVELER 2: Eshu caused a lot of trouble, but he sure enjoyed it.

GRIOT: That's the way of the Trickster—whether he be a god, like Eshu, or a spider, a lion, a hyena, an elephant, a human being—or even a rabbit.

TRAVELER 1: A rabbit! How can an animal play tricks on people?

GRIOT: Well, these *are* myths, but generally animals trick other animals.

TRAVELER 1: For instance, can you give us an example?

GRIOT: The spider Ture tricked a man-eating monster that had lured many curious people into a big, double-sided gong. Once the curious people were inside the gong, they were trapped, and then the monster ate them.

TRAVELER 1: Oh—that *is* crafty.

GRIOT: Ture the Trickster, however, just *pretended* to be curious. He told the monster, "I think I'll climb into your gong—just to see how it works." But when he climbed in, he very carefully left his arm sticking out.

TRAVELER 2: His arm? Oh, so the monster couldn't close the gong.

GRIOT: Exactly. Ture then persuaded the monster to show him "how to climb into the gong properly." Not suspecting a trick, the monster climbed in.

13

TRIBAL CHORUS:	Bang!
TRAVELER 1:	Bang! Ture closed the gong! (*Pause*) Now the monster was dead, right?
TRAVELER 2:	You've got it! Hey, doesn't this spider Ture remind you of a certain Trickster we know?
TRAVELER 1:	I don't know any hyenas or spiders or elephants—maybe a rabbit?
TRAVELER 2:	Yes, a rabbit—Brer Rabbit.
GRIOT:	Some say the stories about Brer Rabbit have roots deep down in our myths—African myths. I believe that! Makes sense to me!
TRAVELER 1:	I've read lots of those stories. Tar Baby is my favorite one.
TRIBAL CHORUS:	Yes, yes!
TRAVELER 2:	I have to read some of those again—maybe learn a trick or two, huh?
GRIOT:	You might. For sure, I'd call Brer Rabbit a prize Trickster Rabbit!
ESHU:	Not bad. Still, let's keep in touch. I'll keep my eye on you all—and don't forget—rub a little palm oil on my shrine twice a week. Okay? (*Pause*) I'll be watching. Just thought I'd warn you! (*Laughs*)
TRIBAL CHORUS:	Ohhh, no! Eshu!
VENDOR:	(*Shakes both bags*) Chocolate, anyone?
TRIBAL CHORUS:	Yaay! Chocolate! Yaay!

Myths from Around the World: American Indian

Passing the Torch

INTRODUCTION

Opening every new book, we begin our own imaginative "Voyage of Discovery," and when we're transported into the myths of an American Indian people, like the Chinooks, we are sure to discover a land of ancient beliefs that continue even today.

Reading Chinook mythology, we see how completely these early inhabitants of the great Northwest embraced their land and its waters. The Columbia River, which flows through present-day Oregon and Washington, nurtured them for centuries. Fish such as salmon and sturgeon provided both food and a means of livelihood. Surrounding forests of pine and cedar supported animals such as deer, elk, and bears, which early on provided food, clothing, and shelter.

The Chinook people traded many of their goods and crafts with neighboring tribes, but in the early 1800s new markets opened up. Traders and entrepreneurs from other lands came seeking the lush furs, particularly the beaver pelts that were in great demand abroad and available here. The Chinooks, friendly and adaptable as traders, went a step further for their trading partners. They incorporated a working knowledge of English and French into their own vocabulary. This simplified language became known as *Chinook jargon*, a useful skill that was used in conversation and trading.

Unfortunately, much of the original Chinook land was taken over by government acquisitions and modern dams, and tragically, many of the Chinook people have died, victims of diseases spread by our so-called modern civilization. The myths, though, live on, reminding us of a proud heritage and enriching the Chinook people of today.

PRODUCTION NOTES

The spectacular wilderness of the great Northwest has inspired us as a nation ever since the famous Voyage of the Corps of Discovery led by Meriwether Lewis and William Clark. Landscapes, mammals, fish, birds, and people are all grand subjects for reading and writing about and interpreting visually. The Chinook myth that follows pays homage to this land and its inhabitants through oral expression.

The script calls for fourteen boys. (Girls could be used for Sounds A and B.) Fifteen scripts will be required, which includes one for the teacher.

The characters of Lewis and Clark represent our exploring students who travel into this land of the myth. They, of course, speak in standard English.

Blue Jay and Robin, characters from the myth, act as our storytellers. In the myth, they appear as Chinooks *and* as birds. Their language is a variation of Standard English. They use basic, elementary words to tell the tale.

Thunderer, Giant, and Brothers 1, 2, 3, 4, and 5 are all characters in the basic myth. We are using Standard English for the dramatization of their parts in the myth.

Godlike aspects of the mythical characters appear throughout the story. Their transitions from one form to another are somewhat vague, somewhat mysterious, but evil certainly is apparent, as is the power to control it.

For extra fun, here are a few examples of Chinook jargon:

Amusement: he-he	Ocean: hyas salt chuck	Yes: ah-ha'
Big: hy-as	Potato: wap-pa-too'	No: wa'ke
Biscuit: la bis-quee'	Salmon: samon	Pain/disapproval: a-nah
Box: la-ca-sett'	Suppose: spose	Ague: cole-sick
Buffalo: moos-moos	Thank you: mas-say	Bad: me-sah'-che
Drink: muck-a-muck chuck	Watch: tik-tik	Boat: boat
Elk: mool-look	Whale: kwah-nice	Bed: bed

Passing the Torch

Passing the Torch

A Chinook Indian Myth

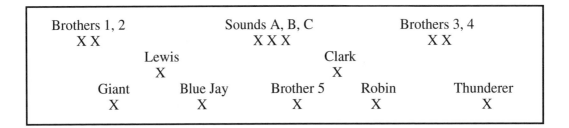

Brothers 1, 2		Sounds A, B, C		Brothers 3, 4	
X X		X X X		X X	
	Lewis		Clark		
	X		X		
Giant	Blue Jay	Brother 5	Robin	Thunderer	
X	X	X	X	X	

SOUNDS A, B, C: (*Four feet march in rhythm until whistle blows and Lewis cries "Halt!"*)

LEWIS: Halt! We'll stop here and make camp for the night.

CLARK: Cap'n Meriwether Lewis—Sir! I don't want to sound disrespectful, but did we have to *march*? We're in the wilderness—three thousand miles from the Missouri—five thousand, I reckon, from Mr. Jefferson.

LEWIS: Point taken, Captain Clark, but tired as we may be, we must keep up appearances. The Chinooks are little different from any of the other tribes we've met. They deserve our full attention.

CLARK: I agree. Their scouts have been most helpful, hospitable—and bearers of food!

LEWIS: They speak pretty good English, too—a kind of Chinook jargon.

CLARK: Sure beats what I know. They've learned a whole 'nother language.

SOUNDS A, B: (*Begin gusts of wind, tree branches rustling, and frantic bird sounds.*)

LEWIS: Say—something's happening to the weather. Look at that river—huge whitecaps, like the ocean!

BLUE JAY: Oh, no, White Man. Not Pacific Ocean—you see big Chinook river!

LEWIS: Of course—that's still the Columbia. Yes, it's a big river—boiling!

CLARK: (*Whispers*) It's a Chinook! I didn't see him coming—or hear him!

LEWIS: (*Whispers*) Sh. Neither did I. (*Aloud*) Must be a storm blowing in.

BLUE JAY: No. No storm. That our god Thunderer—god very angry. I know. (*Thumps chest*) I am Blue Jay. I welcome you to Chinook land.

LEWIS: (*Whispers*) Offer to shake hands, Clark. (*Aloud*) Thank you, Blue Jay. We appreciate that. Ah, who is that with you—is that Thunderer?

BLUE JAY: No. No! Not god Thunderer. Is my brother, called Robin.

LEWIS: Robin—and Blue Jay. I see. Very good. (*Pause*) Ah, your people have been most generous with us. We thank you.

CLARK: Delicious salmon—and that *wappato*, like a baked potato back home in St. Louis. The men really enjoyed it. Many thanks! (*wap-pa-too'*)

SOUNDS A, B: (*Wind, rustling of branches, and bird chirps slowly quiet down and stop.*)

LEWIS: Storm's blowing away, and the river's quiet. Strange phenomenon. Did the god Thunderer cause that? Could you tell us about him?

ROBIN: Starts long time past, (*Pause*) when five brothers live in one small hut.

BLUE JAY: Is long, long story. You listen. Big brother—big boss. Listen, him!

BROTHER 1: It's time, brothers! Sun burns high. Time to fish, to start the hunt.

BROTHER 2: Do you fish today, brother, or do you hunt for game again?

BROTHER 3: Not another elk! That last one was too old and tough. Salmon's better.

BROTHER 1: Or squirrel, then? Perhaps a squirrel. They're good for stew.

BROTHER 4: I'm trying for one of those plump turkeys that parade around here.

BROTHER 5: Let me go with you, please? My arrows can fly fast and straight—just like yours. (*Pause*) I don't like staying home, doing squaw's work!

BROTHER 2: Your time will come, little brother. Be patient.

BROTHER 3: And work hard in the garden. That's your task, too.

BROTHER 4: And lay in plenty of firewood, little brother. If my hunting goes well, we'll have roast turkey tonight. We'll see you when night falls.

BLUE JAY: So four big brothers go to river and fish for salmon and out to forest and hunt meat for winter. Little brother stays home.

ROBIN: All alone. Very sad, too.

BLUE JAY: (*Laughs slyly*) But soon not alone! Big giant breaks into hut!

SOUNDS A, B: (*Huge crashing noises from pots and pans*)

GIANT: (*Big voice*) Nothing? Nothing is here! You, there, boy, *fetch me food*!

BROTHER 5: (*Stammering*) A giant! How did you get in here? Who . . . who are you?

GIANT: Don't question me, boy. *Fetch me food!*

ROBIN:	Strange giant very huge. Big giant head hit rafters of hut like giant tree. Big hairy feet like black bear from forest, from mountain.
BLUE JAY:	Big hands like wild panther. Pick up little brother, shake him and shake him, like small dog.
ROBIN:	Little brother see giant's fat belly. Feed that?!! He very scared!
BROTHER 5:	Oh, what should I do? Feed him? He's a monster! He will eat up all our food! (*Pause*) But if I don't feed him, then what?
SOUNDS A, B:	(*Pans bang. Dishes rattle. Pounding on table.*)
GIANT:	Bring that food to me now! I know you have it, boy. I can *smell* it.
BLUE JAY:	So young boy brings out more and more food, and giant eat and eat all day long. Deer, elk, squirrel—all disappear into mouth of ugly monster.
ROBIN:	Night comes. Four big brothers come back to hut. Go inside—see giant—hear giant hit table, hear him shout many times for more food.
GIANT:	Bring me those turkeys, and that fresh meat. Where's the salmon?
BROTHER 5:	(*Loud whisper*) Oh, brothers, do as he says. Do it! He's a monster—he's evil—and he's huge!
BROTHER 4:	He has eaten all our supplies for the winter, and now he's eating all the meat from our hunt today! So when that is gone, then what?
BROTHER 3:	(*Whispers*) Let me ask. (*Pause*) Uh, sir, we're running low on food. And we're wondering—what will you do when all our food is gone?

GIANT: (*Deep, evil laugh*) What shall I eat when nothing's left but these skins and hides and you? (*Another deep, threatening laugh*) I think you know! (*Pause. Yawns*) I sleep now. When I wake, I must be fed, with whatever or whoever is in front of me. And don't try to leave—I am sleeping here, in front of the door. You can't get out!

SOUND A: (*Snoring begins. Occasional bouts of snoring punctuate next six speeches.*)

BROTHER 2: (*Whispers*) He's out like a candle! Plan something, brothers!

BROTHER 1: I have it! He wouldn't eat the skins and hides tonight, but if we boil them well, like a stew, maybe he'll eat them in the morning.

BROTHER 3: Good idea, but then what? Once he eats the skins, then what? Us?

BROTHER 4: (*Little laugh*) Not us—not if we're not here!

BROTHER 5: You mean run away? But we can't! He's sleeping in front of the door.

BROTHER 2: But we must get out! And I know how—we make a hole in the roof!

BROTHER 4: Excellent. That will work! Now, look outside. Watch for the moon. By the time it rises, the skins will be cooked, and we will be ready!

SOUNDS A, C: (*Snoring stops. Dog begins to yip.*)

BROTHER 1: Hush! Hush! Good dog. (*Conspiring*) Now, Spot, when the giant asks you where we've gone, you must point him down the wrong road.

SOUND C: (*Dog barks "okay."*)

BROTHER 1: Everyone, be ready. The sky grows brighter. The moon is on the rise!

BLUE JAY: One by one, all brothers escape through hole in roof! They run fast.

ROBIN: But daytime comes through hole in roof! Giant wakes. Brothers gone!

GIANT: Dog! Dog! Which way did they go? This way? Down this road?

ROBIN: Dog shakes head. He points nose other way. Giant goes down wrong road. No brothers. Mad. Mad! Three times he asks dog. More wrong roads. Does not find brothers. *But* on fourth try, he sees them.

BLUE JAY: They run and run, but brothers cannot escape big steps of angry giant.

ROBIN: Giant catch one big brother. Kills him dead. Then, next three—killed.

CLARK: All four of them? What happened to the youngest brother?

LEWIS: Surely one got away. Besides, we haven't met the god Thunderer yet.

BLUE JAY: No. You very wise. Long story. Now, little brother very afraid. Must escape! Boy runs on and on, to big river. Man there on shore, fishing.

BROTHER 5: (*Panting*) Excuse me, sir, I see you have a small boat. Please, will you take me across the river? Something is chasing me. I must escape!

THUNDERER: What's the matter with you, boy? The salmon are running today!

BROTHER 5: But, sir, the monster—the giant glutton—he's after me!

ROBIN: Man frowns at "giant glutton." He pulls in net. Then rows boy across.

THUNDERER: All right, boy, now do as I say. Follow that path through the forest until you come to my hut. Go in. You stay there. I will return.

BLUE JAY: Fisherman goes back to salmon nets and sees evil giant glutton.

23

GIANT: You, there! You with the boat! Take me across this river!

THUNDERER: Can't do it. Salmon are running today. My net's filling up. I'm busy.

GIANT: (*Wheedling*) Look here, fellow, fishermen always need more twine. Suppose you take me across, and I give you this hank of twine.

THUNDERER: Well, I'm not sure my boat will hold both of us. But I will stretch myself across the river, and you may walk across on my body.

GIANT: (*Impatient*) Whatever you say. I must get across this river!

BLUE JAY: Fisherman stretch himself clear across river. Giant slap hat on head and step onto feet of fisherman. Then giant start to walk up legs.

ROBIN: Oh, ho! fisherman move legs far apart. Giant wobbles—going to fall! Giant monster scared! Grow very green in face! He shake and holler!

GIANT: You tricked me, you—! You tricked me! Help, help! I'm falling!

BLUE JAY: (*Small laugh*) Nobody—no thing going save him. Giant falls in cold river water. His hat falls, too. They both float away and disappear.

THUNDERER: I will not save you. You are Evil. Only when storms begin to rage will you ever be heard.

LEWIS: That fisherman—could that be the god Thunderer?

CLARK: Has to be! But what happens to the young brother sent to the hut?

BLUE JAY: Good! Fisherman—god Thunderer—returns to hut. Young brother there. Time pass. Young brother marries daughter of Thunderer.

ROBIN: God Thunderer now father-in-law. Family now. All live in same hut.

24

LEWIS: I have a feeling this story goes on.

ROBIN: Two sons born. Thunderer now grandfather—but story becomes sad. You gonna see.

BROTHER 5: Good morning, Wife. I see that your father is out fishing for whales today. That's a very tough job. I want to go to the sea and watch him.

BLUE JAY: Young man's wife says, "Not go! Father want *nobody* watch him!"

ROBIN: Young man frowns, but he goes to seashore and finds father-in-law fighting big, very big whale. Sees old man lose whale.

BLUE JAY: Thunderer sees son-in-law watching. Very angry! Makes big storm come. Thunder! Lightning! Old man starts for home. Son-in-law, too.

CLARK: That was a pretty strong reaction. How does the son-in-law take that?

BLUE JAY: You listen: On way home, son-in-law finds small piece black coal, climbs big mountain, makes face all black with coal. (*Blows big gust*) Big blow! Big winds! Bad! Everything blow away, even small hut.

LEWIS: So, the son-in-law causes the storm. *He* seems to have power now.

BLUE JAY: Wife knows. Father knows: torch is dying. So he let son-in-law watch him fish again for whales. But listen, son-in-law feels *his* power now.

ROBIN: Young man move fast. Washes black coal off face—and storm stops! (*Pause*) Now young man has message for father-in-law!

BROTHER 5: In the morning, I will go down to the sea to fish for whales. You come, too, Father-in-law. *This* time, you will see *me* catching whales.

BLUE JAY: They go. Young man throws net into sea, and net catches big, big whale. Young man pulls in net, grabs big whale, and throws whale on seashore, at feet of father-in-law.

THUNDERER: (*Deep, rolling laughter*) Gods be praised! It's my son-in-law! He is just like I was!

ROBIN: Time pass more. Daughter has two sons. Old god Thunderer restless.

THUNDERER: Come here, Son-in-law. Time grows heavy for me. I need my friends from the forest, my old playmates. Fetch my two wolves for me.

BLUE JAY: Son-in-law obeys. Goes to forest and brings back two wolves to god Thunderer. But listen—wolves not playmates now. Thunderer weak.

SOUNDS B, C: (*Wolf noises: gnarling and yipping*)

THUNDERER: Stop! Stop! Remember me! I am god Thunderer! Remember me!

SOUNDS B, C: (*Wolf noises: ferocious gnarling and barking*)

THUNDERER: Son-in-law! Son-in-law, take them back!

SOUNDS B, C: (*Wolf noises die away.*)

THUNDERER: They've forgotten how we played, years ago. But, wait! The *bears* will remember. Son-in-law, go deep into the forest. Find my friends, two brown bears I played with when I was a boy. Oh, I miss them so.

BLUE JAY: Again, son-in-law is good. He finds the two bears, and brings bears to Thunderer. Thunderer happy, but bears forget *him*. They fight him!

SOUNDS B, C: (*Bear noises: loud, deep growling*)

THUNDERER: No! Remember! Remember! We are friends. Friends!

SOUNDS B, C: (*Bear noises grow louder, more threatening.*)

BROTHER 5: What would you have me do with the bears, Father-in-law?

THUNDERER: Stop them! Take them away. Take them back to the forest!

SOUNDS B, C: (*Bear noises fade away.*)

THUNDERER: (*Weary*) Ah, what is happening? Son-in-law, go to the forest. Find the two big grizzly bears I knew long ago. Bring them to me.

BLUE JAY: Son-in-law goes deep into forest. Finds two grizzly bears.

BROTHER 5: Come, bears. Come with me. I must take you to Thunderer.

ROBIN: Grizzly bears listen to son-in-law and follow him, but same thing again. *They* forget Thunderer, too. Now, Thunderer has new plan.

THUNDERER: Son-in-law, I have a different task for you. You see this log of wood?

BROTHER 5: Yes. It's from the giant cedar tree I cut down yesterday.

THUNDERER: Good. Take your axe and cut a long split down the log.

BROTHER 5: I will obey you, Father-in-law, but the log is hollow.

THUNDERER: (*Laughs*) I know. Do as I ask!

BLUE JAY: Son-in-law does what he is told. Then Thunderer makes bold move!

THUNDERER: Step inside the log, my boy. Let us see how strong you are.

BLUE JAY: Son-in-law obeys. No fear. He steps inside, and Thunderer closes wood tight around him. Then Thunderer leaves him, walks away.

ROBIN: But son-in-law strong! Takes one big breath, and log breaks open. Danger gone. Son-in-law picks up heavy log and starts for home.

BLUE JAY: He comes to hut and drops big log outside. Ground begins rumble—angry shake—feels like bad earthquake. Thunderer speaks.

THUNDERER: Oh, my son-in-law, you are just as I was when I was a young man!

CLARK: All these tests to obey—to find courage and strength. Why?

LEWIS: Well, Thunderer seems to grow older, yet he still tests the young man.

BLUE JAY: Many tales here—not over yet. I know. I suffer pain from Thunderer.

ROBIN: Thunderer demand more from son-in-law. Next, two strange journeys.

THUNDERER: Son-in-law, I have a task for you. You must go to the land of the Supernatural Folk and bring me their shiny hoops.

BROTHER 5: Hoops? Well, I found the Supernatural Folk. They were playing with a large, shiny hoop, but their land was so bright, it dazzled my eyes. I waited until darkness fell. Then I stole their hoop. But the Supernatural Folk saw me and chased me with burning sticks of fire.

BLUE JAY: Now wife must do something! Calls to children to whip grandfather!

ROBIN: They whip Thunderer again and again. Old grandfather cries and cries. Tears pour down on burning sticks of fire. Son-in-law saved!

BLUE JAY: Same bad thing happen to son-in-law in land of Spirit Folk. But again, Thunderer punished with whip, and again, tears save son-in-law.

BROTHER 5: Time hangs heavy now. I must seek adventure on my own. Perhaps I will challenge the chief in that far-off village to a shooting match.

BLUE JAY: (*Angry*) My village! Fight my chief? No! The adventurer will not live!

BROTHER 5: That Trickster was right! I lost the match. Because of Blue Jay, I lost!

BLUE JAY: (*Furious*) I sprang upon him—I tore off his hair, and cut off his head!

ROBIN: But, no die! Son-in-law goes into deep, deep death-sleep for many months. Two old women feed him, care for him.

BLUE JAY: Finally sons come and look everywhere for their father. Then, sons find me. Sons look at me, and my hair bursts into flames. I fly to village chief. I shout, "The sons! The sons! They're more powerful than we!"

BROTHER 5: My sons destroyed Blue Jay, and they brought me back to life. They set up peace and order in the village. Then we started for home.

CLARK: So, what happens to Thunderer? (*Pause*) Blue Jay? (*Pause*) Robin?

SOUNDS A, B, C: (*Rustle of branches; gusts of wind; a few fading bird sounds*)

LEWIS: They've disappeared, Cap'n Clark—gone, like Thunderer perhaps.

CLARK: Am I missing something—like, is there a moral to this story?

LEWIS: It's a myth about fear and power and evil. Thunderer overcomes the evil giant. The young brother loses his fears and gains strength and courage and power. Then Evil appears again, and the wife and sons take over. But Evil's done for now. The torch of power has been passed. (*Pause*) Are you ready, Captain Clark? Shall we march on?

SOUNDS A, B, C: (*Birds chirp. Winds blow. Then all are silent. Whistle blows.*)

Myths from Around the World: American Indian

Captured!

INTRODUCTION

The great Southwest of America, home of the Pueblo people, is a land of both hardship and enchantment. The climate can be unforgiving—hot and dry or bitterly cold. The terrain ranges from broad deserts to mountains, green with forests and rich with life-giving plants. Here, the Pueblo Indians have spun a mythic culture that entertains, yet underscores a host of moral values that direct their lives.

The very word *pueblo* (Spanish for town or village) identifies these people. They have been close-knit for centuries, ever adapting to this beautiful, mysterious, harsh land. Living close together, they share the bounties of the land as well as its hazards, for the scarcity of water and the dangers of wild animals can be a constant threat.

In the myths, however, wild animals, birds, and fish often serve to define the nature of good and evil. For example, the coyote, homeless and predatory, often exemplifies trickery and stupidity in humans. We can also find explanations in the myth for the origin of the world and all things in it. For example, where do arrowheads come from? Ah, the myth says the horned toad with its jagged back invented the arrowheads.

In addition to these observations and speculations, the Pueblo stories emphasize moral codes of industry, obedience, truthfulness, and bravery. Then, overseeing this whole complex world are the gods, the Trues.

From simple caves to skillfully handcrafted multilevel homes, some perched on the top of forbidding mesas, the Pueblo people developed and still maintain a strong identity with a life of purpose that envelops a whole community.

PRODUCTION NOTES

Some ancestors of the Pueblo people date clear back to 3000 B.C. Today, modern inhabitants of the Southwest continue to refine their ancient, inherited arts that reflect the mysterious beauty of this land. Sunsets, mountains, deserts, cacti—all are subjects for today's artistic outpourings in forms such as pottery, sculpture, painting, and weaving. Both modern literature and the vivid myths from ancient storytellers add to these arts and crafts.

"Captured!" is one such story. Our script calls for a cast and crew of eleven students. Twelve script copies are needed, which includes one for the teacher.

Three animals (anthropomorphized) act as the narrators:

Mole is sometimes cantankerous and disbelieving.

Toad is cool—he's on top of things!

Coyote, however, displays fear and cowardice, even whining at times.

Castor and Pollux, hero twins, and their Father are humanlike protagonists.

Witch Wife and Witch Husband represent evil forces that attack Castor and Pollux when they disobey the rules. Witch Wife, not a melodious female role, can easily be played by a versatile boy. She cackles. She bosses. She connives. She's in charge!

The Sun god is one god (like the Trues) who protects the hero twins.

Sound effects include simple piping (from a reed pipe, perhaps), bird chirpings, fists pounding, a knife chipping a hard surface, feet running, sticks hitting wood, and two body thuds (the Witch Wife and Witch Husband).

Any or all of these sound effects can be eliminated, but invention can be fun!

Captured!

Captured!

A Pueblo Indian Myth

	Sun			Sounds A, B			Witch Husband	
	X			X X			X	
Castor	Pollux		Toad	Mole	Coyote		Father	Witch Wife
X	X		X	X	X		X	X

SOUNDS A, B: (*Soft tune from reed pipe; intermittent bird calls*)

MOLE: What's going on, Toad? Noise! Too much noise!

TOAD: For a mole, maybe. With those eyes of yours, you can't know what a glorious day this is. New Mexico may be dry and warm, but I don't want to be anywhere else.

MOLE: You want to sing about this? Oh, go jump in the Rio Grande!

COYOTE: Not another argument, guys, please! It's my toothache! People-talk is enough already!

TOAD: It's not all about you, Coyote! Listen, they're moving, you know, the Pueblo People, and they're taking the boys with them.

MOLE: Well, of course! If those twin boys are really sons of the Sun god, they *need* taking care of.

COYOTE: I wish *I* had a real home. Maybe I could visit them.

TOAD: Fat chance! They're leaving the village for a little ranch. The father wants to train them to be great hunters. I've heard him say so.

COYOTE: Let me guess—therein lies a tale! So, start the story, Toad. Go!

SOUNDS A, B: (*Brief soft tune from reed pipe; brief bird calls*)

FATHER: Eh, boys—never leave your hunting quivers out at night. The leather will become dusty, and then your arrows will fall useless to the ground. Every good hunter must protect his weapons. Understand?

CASTOR: Yes, Father. We understand.

POLLUX: It was a mistake, Father. We'll be careful.

FATHER: Good. Now, the plan for today: Hunt for rabbits, again. Use your eyes well. You may hunt as far as the mountains, hunt to the east, the west, and the north, but do not—I repeat—do not travel to the south.

CASTOR: But why not south, Father?

FATHER: It is not safe! Do not question me!

POLLUX: Yes, Father. We'll start out now—and hunt farther west.

TOAD: Let's follow along. (*Pause*) I trust you're all ready? Excellent. So the next day, the twins went hunting again—to the east and the north. They were successful, but the rabbits were harder and harder to find.

CASTOR: Whew! I'm about worn out. We've covered this land every day for weeks. And what do we have to show for it?

POLLUX: Not much. And I don't think it's us. We're not missing our aim. We are just not finding any rabbits out here.

CASTOR: You're right. The rabbits have left these parts. They've gone south.

POLLUX: South? You may be right. So, why don't we follow them?

CASTOR:	You know why. Father warned us. Told us not to go there.
POLLUX:	We don't have to stay. Come on. Let's go south for just one day.
MOLE:	Ah, the temptation was too great. What could possibly happen?
CASTOR:	Wow! Look at the string of rabbits we've got! Staying out of the south makes no sense at all. We haven't had a bit of trouble!
WITCH WIFE:	(*Cackles*) Well, well. Someone's been hunting on my land.
POLLUX:	(*Whispers*) Castor! Look at that—that *thing*! Is she a . . . a *witch*?
CASTOR:	Oh, sorry, Grandmother. We didn't know it was your land.
POLLUX:	We've only taken down a few rabbits. Would you like them back?
WITCH WIFE:	(*Cackles*) No. No, we don't eat *rabbits*. (*Pause*) But I see that you must. And that you like to hunt. Perfect. Come with me.
COYOTE:	Oh, they shouldn't do that! She's scary!
MOLE:	You are such a coward! But you're right. She's a real Witch Wife.
WITCH WIFE:	Come, boys. Jump into this nice big basket of mine. I will take you to my house, where you can hunt for rabbits all day long.
CASTOR:	(*Whispers*) Brother, she is so ugly! See those warts? I'm not going.
POLLUX:	(*Whispers*) We don't have a choice now. We'll escape later.
COYOTE:	Fat chance of that. I've seen her hut—and her ugly old husband.

WITCH WIFE: Jump in, boys—we have a long way to go.

TOAD: The way was long and hard and rocky, but the Witch Wife carried the boys all the way in her big straw basket. Finally, when night fell, she stopped. They had arrived.

CASTOR: (*Whispers*) I suppose this is it—look at that hovel! It's a wreck!

POLLUX: (*Whispers*) If she takes us in that shack, I know we can break out.

WITCH WIFE: Step down, boys, and don't move. (*Cackles*) It won't do you any good. There's no trail out of here—and no people—just my husband, and he'll not help you. (*Cackles*) He's much too fond of boy-meat!

CASTOR: (*Whispers*) Brother, what do you think she means by *boy-meat*?

POLLUX: (*Whispers*) I don't know, but it makes my blood curdle. We're in trouble, and there's no way out of this place.

WITCH WIFE: (*Calling*) Husband! You in there! Husband! Come out here! Get busy!

WITCH HUSBAND: (*Surly*) Must you always yell at me? I'm not deaf! What do you want?

WITCH WIFE: Build up the fire for the oven! A big fire, one that will last all night.

WITCH HUSBAND: Whatever for? Another of your harebrained schemes?

WITCH WIFE: (*Cackles a laugh*) Harebrained? Oh, that's good, very good. *No!*

WITCH HUSBAND: No lucky rabbits, eh? Then what?

WITCH WIFE: (*Coyly*) I could make you guess—but on the other hand, take a look.

WITCH HUSBAND:	Ye gods! I see two young boys. (*Pause*) Boys! Wife, do you mean . . . ?
WITCH WIFE:	Of course! Boy-meat done to perfection in the outdoor *horno*. That means gathering a lot of wood and building a *big fire*—and that means you! So get busy. Be good for *something* for a change.
WITCH HUSBAND:	I'm going. I'm going! Now, you do your part, Wife!
COYOTE:	Oh, Toad, I don't like the sound of this. Bad. Really, really bad.
TOAD:	(*Sigh*) Man, you are so astute! What a clever coyote. "It looks bad."
MOLE:	This time, Coyote's right, Toad. I can feel the heat from this fire. The *horno's* blazing hot, ready to bake bread, or *something*.
WITCH HUSBAND:	All right, Wife. Are you happy now?
WITCH WIFE:	Well, you've done your job, but there's still plenty of work for me. Get me my rake. I need to smooth out those hot coals. Move!
CASTOR:	Why is she looking at us like that, Brother? (*Pause*) Hey! Look out! She's trying to grab you! Run, Brother, run!
POLLUX:	I can't! Grandmother, let go! Let go! Stop! You're hurting my arm.
WITCH WIFE:	Come, boy. It's just a game. You, too, boy—crawl into my oven, and be quick about it! (*Calling*) Husband, come here. They're in!
WITCH HUSBAND:	What's the rush? I'm expecting *well-done* boy-meat, plump and juicy.
WITCH WIFE:	Don't be an idiot. Hand me those flat stones so I can close up the oven. Then, bring a basket of wet clay. I must seal the stones good—those at the front of the oven and over the smoke hole. Now, move!
CASTOR:	(*Muffled objections*) Wait, Grandmother. Wait!

POLLUX:	Let us out of here! *Help, help*! We're roasting! Help!
SOUND A:	(*Frantic pounding with fists on drum top*)
WITCH WIFE:	(*Cackles*) Pound all you like, my dearies. Pound away. The door is sealed, and the coals are just right for roasting wild young boys!
WITCH HUSBAND:	Come, Wife. It is time for bed, and time to dream about our breakfast.
WITCH WIFE:	(*Cackles*) Breakfast—yes! Which part of the meat do you like best?
WITCH HUSBAND:	I'm not particular, Dear heart. You can choose first.
WITCH WIFE:	Thank you, Husband. All of it will be a feast, I'm sure—that is, once the heat goes down and the carving takes place. I can hardly wait!
SOUND A:	(*Pounding lessens, but continues sporadically.*)
POLLUX:	It's no use! Give it up, Castor!
CASTOR:	No! We cannot be defeated by that evil witch, but we need help!
POLLUX:	I know that! But no one knows we're here. Who can help?
CASTOR:	The Trues. We have to appeal to the Trues. We must pray to them.
POLLUX:	The Trues? What makes you think the gods will help us?
CASTOR:	I don't know if they will, but we must try! Now, pray, hard!
SOUND A:	(*Immediately, the pounding stops.*)
SOUND B:	(*Soft notes played on reed whistle or flute; silence; hands clap*)
WITCH HUSBAND:	Hurry up, Wife. Daylight's upon us, and I need my breakfast.

WITCH WIFE:	You're hungry, eh? Might you be tempted by a small chunk of fresh-roasted boy-meat?
WITCH HUSBAND:	I would indeed. Why are you standing here, asking stupid questions? Open up that oven of yours, and let's see what we've got.
WITCH WIFE:	All right, all right! Start chipping away that hard clay.
SOUND A:	(*Chipping on hard surface, such as ice or a rock*)
WITCH HUSBAND:	This is not easy, Wife, but the top stone's loose. Smoke hole's free.
WITCH WIFE:	Well, get on with it. No, give me the knife. I'll break open the door.
SOUND A:	(*Chipping continues*)
CASTOR:	(*Laughing*) Hey, you're it, little brother!
POLLUX:	You can't tag me! I got you first!
WITCH WIFE:	What's going on? What's happened? Why, they're not roasted at all.
SOUND A:	(*Knife or chisel and rocks crash to the ground.*)
WITCH WIFE:	They're *playing!* They're *alive!* (*Pause*) Husband! It's your fault. You didn't build a hot enough fire. You have to do it again—now!
CASTOR:	(*Whispers*) Listen! The door's open. Let's get out of this oven!
POLLUX:	(*Whispers*) I'm right behind you. Go!
SOUNDS A, B:	(*Feet running*)
CASTOR:	(*Panting*) Run faster, Pollux, faster!
POLLUX:	(*Panting*) We're safe, Brother. Slow down. It was the gods. The Trues heard us. They saved us from that heat! We need to give thanks!
CASTOR:	I have. Soon as I heard that chipping, I sent up thanks for both of us.

WITCH WIFE: (*Cackle*) Oh, boys, boys! Over here, boys.

SOUNDS A, B: (*Running stops.*)

POLLUX: (*Whispers*) It's the Witch Woman! How did she catch up with us?

WITCH WIFE: Stop where you are, boys. I have a present for you.

POLLUX: (*Mutters*) Oh, great. A present from a witch!

WITCH WIFE: See? I've brought you your bows and arrows. You can go hunting.

CASTOR: Thank you, Grandmother. Where *can* we go hunting?

WITCH WIFE: Why, right here in the forest, young man. You don't want to go too far away. I wouldn't want you to get too tired. That's not good for your muscles. Besides, there is *no other place* where you can go.

MOLE: (*Surprised*) She's going to keep them there?

TOAD: Of course. She's hungry. The old man is hungry. They can just about taste that boy-meat!

COYOTE: I see. Now the old husband has to build another fire.

TOAD: Right—and imprison the twins, seal up the oven again—and wait.

MOLE: But maybe that boy-roasting doesn't work this time, either.

COYOTE: Does the Witch Wife finally give up then?

TOAD: You are so naïve! Three times the Witch Wife and her husband try. But no matter how hot the fire grows, the boys always emerge from the oven unharmed. They have the Trues, their gods, on their side.

MOLE: But the witch must be furious by now. The coals will have burned down, right? The Witch Wife will have to dream up a new scheme.

41

WITCH WIFE: Did you boys have a good time today shooting arrows at the rabbits?

CASTOR: Yes, Grandmother.

WITCH WIFE: Oh, that is good, but I have another game for you to play. Ready?

POLLUX: Yes, Grandmother. (*Pause*) I sort of hope it's better than the last one.

WITCH WIFE: (*Cackles*) Oh, you already know a version of this game. *We* call it Nah-oo-pah-chee. *You* call it hide-and seek. You do know it?

CASTOR: Sure, we know it, Grandmother.

WITCH WIFE: Good. Here are the rules. Listen to me: in Nah-hoo-pah-chee, we take turns hiding. Now, whoever is found *three* times shall be the loser of this game and must pay with his life.

COYOTE: Oh, I'd get out of that game.

TOAD: Maybe you would, but these twin boys can't. The Witch Woman has challenged them. They can't refuse. It would not be honorable.

WITCH WIFE: If we are agreed, then, good night. In the morning we will begin playing Nah-oo-pah-chee. (*Cackle*) Pleasant dreams.

POLLUX: (*Whispers*) Castor, are you thinking what I'm thinking?

CASTOR: (*Whispers*) The Trues! If the gods don't help us in this game, we'll be cooked, for sure. Pray, Pollux, pray for help!

COYOTE: I don't trust that woman. I think she's a witch!

TOAD: Brilliant, Coyote! Bad things are going to happen in the morning!

WITCH WIFE: Let's begin the game! Boys, you hide first. I will cover my eyes. Go!

CASTOR: (*Whispers*) Over by doorposts, Pollux.

POLLUX: (*Whispers*) I'm going. I only hope the Trues have been listening to us.

SOUND A: (*Stick hits a piece of wood six times to illustrate time passing.*)

WITCH WIFE: Aha! Over by the doorposts, boys. I see you! My turn! You find me!

SOUND A: (*Stick begins hitting piece of wood again.*)

CASTOR: Pollux, we have to cover our eyes, you know.

POLLUX: I'm not looking, but I think I hear her. (*Calls*) Grandmother, come out, come out! You're hiding under that white duck on the lake.

SOUND A: (*Stick stops hitting wood.*)

WITCH WIFE: Curses! How did you find me? Did you peek?

CASTOR: No, Grandmother, just a lucky guess.

POLLUX: That's right. It's our second turn now. Hide your eyes!

SOUND A: (*Stick hits wood again.*)

CASTOR: (*Whispers*) Pollux, what are we going to do? Do you have an idea?

POLLUX: I think so. Make yourself really small. We can hide in our quivers.

WITCH WIFE: Come out, come out—you're hiding in your quivers.

SOUND A: (*Stick stops hitting wood.*)

WITCH WIFE: I found you! But you'll never find me this time! Hide your eyes!

SOUND A: (*Stick begins hitting wood again.*)

CASTOR: We're ready, Grandmother. (*Whispers*) Wait a bit, brother. She's made herself very small. I think I know where she is, though.

POLLUX: (*Whispers*) Okay! (*Pause*) Grandmother, Grandmother, come out, come out. We see you behind the foot of the big crane near the lake.

SOUND A: (*Stick stops hitting wood.*)

CASTOR: (*Whispers*) This is our third and last chance, Pollux! Run to father Sun. We must hide there!

SUN: Such foolish sons I have!

POLLUX: I know, Father Sun, but please, please hide us from that witch.

SUN: Quick! Under my right arm. Go! She won't find you there.

MOLE: Now, I have to tell you that the old witch looked everywhere, but she *couldn't* find the boys this time. Were they happy! But the old witch, taking her third turn, went back to the lake and found a giant fish.

SOUND A: (*Stick begins hitting wood again.*)

CASTOR: I don't know where she went—maybe back to the lake.

POLLUX: Hey, look at the bubbles on the lake. Guess what?

CASTOR: Grandmother, come out! We see you. You're hiding in that big fish!

SOUND A: (*Stick stops hitting wood.*)

POLLUX: Remember the agreement, you—you—you, *Witch Wife*!

WITCH WIFE: I remember—but you wouldn't do that. You *wouldn't!*

CASTOR: Sharp arrows, Brother. Careful aim. Shoot!

SOUND B: (*Body falls to the ground.*)

POLLUX: (*Pause*) Good shot. Now for the evil husband!

SOUND A: (*Another body falls to the ground.*)

CASTOR: Well done! I think we're finished with the south.

POLLUX: One thing more. We must replace their hearts with these kernels of corn. They *are* witches, but if they do manage to come back to life, they will come as virtuous people with pure, kind hearts.

CASTOR: Well said, Pollux. Now let us return to the pueblo and find our father.

FATHER: I am already here, sons—and though you disobeyed me, you acted honorably, and I forgive you. (*Proudly*) Furthermore, I must tell you, we are going to have rabbits everywhere. Now we can all hunt in the south, thanks to my sons!

SOUNDS A, B: (*Soft tune from reed pipe. Intermittent bird calls.*)

Myths from Around the World: Arabia

The Quest of Gilgamesh

INTRODUCTION

An ancient poem, *The Epic of Gilgamesh* (the story behind this script) may seem at first glance to be just another Arabian tale. True, this story of the fabled King Gilgamesh contains adventures, but they are more complex than just a story of daring deeds. Richer elements are included, such as the history and geography of Mesopotamia and the moral and spiritual beliefs of an early civilization in the area we now call Iraq.

Early stories about King Gilgamesh appeared first in the Sumerian language nearly four thousand years ago. The most complete versions, in a long poem dated much later, were written in cuneiform on twelve clay tablets. The first modern translation was made in the 1880s, but scholars continue to decipher the surviving tablets and fragments.

The Epic of Gilgamesh is rooted in both myth and history. Mythically, Gilgamesh is presented as being two-thirds god and one-third man. Historically, this king is thought to have ruled in the ancient Mesopotamian city of Uruk about 2700 BC.

Both the humans and the gods in these stories reflect the basic beliefs of these early people. For example, when an overbearing Gilgamesh offends his people, the gods take action, wishing to make him better. The king's subsequent meeting with Enkidu, a different sort of man, begins with an angry confrontation, but in the growing harmony of their relationship, Enkidu becomes more human and King Gilgamesh more humane.

Evil appears, but even destroying evil has its consequence—Enkidu's death. However, Gilgamesh's eventual acceptance of death brings the story to its final truth: It is man's fate to die; therefore, he should live his life to the fullest.

PRODUCTION NOTES

Something exotic, yet biblical, drifts throughout the story of Gilgamesh. It's bigger than life. The characters are of this world, and yet they're not. No wonder, then, that this myth holds such an attraction for us.

47

The following script calls for eleven readers and three crew members. Fifteen scripts will be needed, including one for the teacher.

Elders 1–5 act as narrators for the story, and with their occasional comments, highlight the actions and emotions of the other characters.

Gilgamesh, the king, is above all proud. His emotions range from the regal and commanding to the reckless and defiant. Yet in the end, Gilgamesh's pride evolves from his personal desires for glory to larger hopes for his people.

Enkidu, who is sent by the gods to be a foil for Gilgamesh, begins with great bravado, but his sensibilities begin to outweigh the heedless actions of his "brother," Gilgamesh. It is the tragedy of his death that begins to change the attitudes of the king.

Anu, the chief god, brings a thoughtful presence to the problems of the king.

Humbaba, the guardian of the forest, is strong, loud, and officious.

Urshanabi is a surly boatman who rows Gilgamesh to meet Utnapishtim.

Utnapishtim, a character with experiences from another Great Flood, shows a calm sense of maturity and wisdom.

The sound effects are explained as they are presented throughout the script. They are simple but imaginative additions to the narration and action of the story. Although they are inventive and supportive, they can be eliminated with little harm to the script.

The Quest of Gilgamesh

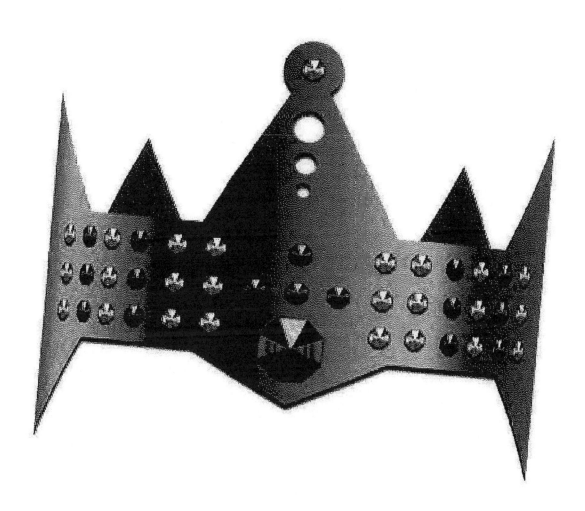

The Quest of Gilgamesh

Pre-Iraqi Myth

Sound A		Sound B			Sound C	
X		X			X	
	Urshanabi	Humbaba		Anu	Utnapishtim	
	X	X		X	X	
Elders 4, 5, 1		Gilgamesh	Enkidu		Elders 2, 3	
X X X		X	X		X X	

GILGAMESH: Welcome to Mesopotamia—and to my city! Greetings to one and all! (*Proudly*) My name is Gilgamesh—*King* Gilgamesh! (*Gill'-ga-mesh*)

SOUNDS A, B, C: (*Chimes tinkle; reed whistle chirps; muffled drumming*)

GILGAMESH: We welcome you, and we commend you to the Elders of this beautiful place! You have entered the gates of our splendid walled city. You have arrived in Uruk. You're home! (*You-ruck'*)

SOUNDS A, B, C: (*Brief flourish of chimes, whistle, and drum. Then silence.*)

ELDERS 4, 5, 1: (*Bow heads briefly. Raise heads. Smile.*) Welcome, all!

ELDER 2: (*Confidentially*) Well, I'd say this was a case of mistaken identity, not to mention time travel. The story of Gilgamesh is more than four thousand years old, and it took place far, far away!

ELDER 3: Ancient city—ancient times. Sounds like an adventure! Let's join in. Turn back the clock. Flip the map.

ELDER 2: What do we know about Arabia? I remember Babylon.

ELDER 3: You're warm. We *are* talking about Mesopotamia, remember.

ELDER 2: Sure. The land between two rivers—the Tigris and the Euphrates. So Uruk was near today's Baghdad? (*Ty'-gris*) (*You-fray'-teez*)

ELDER 1: Brilliant, my friend! Now, here's an idea. Let us be your guides. We will follow the famous quest of King Gilgamesh—part god, part man.

ELDER 4: You may think that strange, the king's mother being a goddess and his father a man. Nope. Their union made him powerful—kingly!

ELDER 5: See, being part god, he has both a strong body and a pleasing face.

ELDER 4: And he has courage, enough for two men!

ELDER 2: With all that, I hope he has good sense.

ELDER 3: Keep hoping. But I'm game. Let's follow along and see for ourselves.

ELDER 1: Excellent! Remember, he has a king's destiny to fulfill. No weak-livered, mealy-mouthed, milk-boned man can do that!

ELDER 4: Yes, but I'm concerned. His attitude is *too* proud. Let's speak to Anu.

ELDER 5: Consult the king of the gods? Hmm. Risky, but a good idea. Let's go.

SOUND B: (*Whistle: five notes to announce Anu*)

ANU: Honored Elders of Uruk, please be seated, and fear not. Speak up.

ELDER 1: It's Gilgamesh, Anu.

ANU: Ah, is it his pride again? (*Pause*) I believe that it's time for your king to meet a new man, one who is also great in prowess and courage.

ELDER 4: (*Stunned*) How can we make that happen?

ANU: Not you. I will speak to the goddess. A drop of water, a pinch of fine Arabian clay, shape, and behold—the man, Enkidu! (*En-ki-du'*)

SOUND B: (*Whistle: a flurry of notes*)

GILGAMESH: Rumors fly swiftly through the desert, rumors that speak of a hairy, beastlike creature that eats and drinks and sleeps with animals.

ELDER 2: Wait! This wild Enkidu is supposed to be a man like Gilgamesh?

ELDER 1: Not with *that* appearance—but you see, the man, Enkidu, changes.

ELDER 5: Thanks to the love and care of a *very* friendly, beautiful woman.

ELDER 4: She's the one who tames him and tells him about Gilgamesh.

ENKIDU: I'm supposed to challenge the king, Gilgamesh? He who brags he is the strongest man in all Uruk? He who takes and does what he wants?

GILGAMESH: (*Arrogantly*) Of course I do as I wish, and I expect my subjects to do as I say—to honor me, especially the beautiful, young brides.

ENKIDU: Bah! Oh, I'd heard about his exploits with young brides. In fact, we met because of one. I stopped Gilgamesh right outside her door.

GILGAMESH: Out of my way, peasant! I claim a king's privilege to enter this room!

ENKIDU: No! Take not another step, King—not a pebble's worth. That bride is not yours! (*Pause*) No? Remove your crown and fight—man to man!

SOUND C: (*Ominous, low drumming during next three speeches*)

GILGAMESH: Animal! You would-be man! Come—strike me, if you can! My fists are ready. Come at me, Creature!

ENKIDU: "Creature," eh? No! Call me Enkidu—and fight me like a man!

ELDER 5: We saw it all. Enkidu spat on the ground. Then he flew at the king!

ELDER 4: The man-creature had the ungodly strength of ten men. The king reeled from his blows and screamed in pain. They fought furiously.

ELDER 2: So the bride escaped as the would-be men, well matched, fought on.

ELDER 3: But after all, who was the winner?

ELDER 1: Neither. Both. The king and Endiku became friends, close as brothers.

ELDER 4: But not long after, they became restless, this unlikely pair of brothers.

ELDER 1: This is true. They were bored. They craved excitement. They needed a mission—something to enrich the tales of the king's destiny.

GILGAMESH: I have it, Enkidu! I have a plan! We must travel to the Great Forest!

ENKIDU: Oh, no, brother. The Great Forest is forbidden, even to a king.

GILGAMESH: But huge, magnificent cedars grow there. I must cut one down. Then, think of my fame—my deeds carved upon the tablets for all time.

ENKIDU: I know that is your destiny—still . . . .

GILGAMESH: Why do you hold back? You will be famous, too. (*Pause*) Wait, Enkidu, are you afraid of the god Enil?

ENKIDU: I'm afraid of the demon Enil controls—the Guardian of the Forest.

GILGAMESH: You are afraid of Humbaba—that simple watchman? I'm not!

ENKIDU: Humbaba is no simple watchman. He can smell you entering his domain, and then he begins to roar. He spews fire and smoke throughout the Forest. I know him. To see him, Gilgamesh, is to see Death.

GILGAMESH: You *are* afraid! Look, I will go first. You follow.

ENKIDU: At least, visit the sun god first. The cedar country belongs to him.

ELDER 1: Gilgamesh did, and the sun god pleaded with him not to go. Counselors of the city cautioned him. His mother warned him, too.

ELDER 4: Gilgamesh listened to them all, but he tossed off their worries. Indeed, he persuaded Enkidu to enter the Great Forest with him.

SOUND C: (*Slow, quiet drumming during next six speeches*)

ELDER 5: Humbaba was not in sight. Gilgamesh cut down a mighty cedar.

ELDER 1: It *crashed* to the ground. Humbaba heard the noise. Another tree fell.

HUMBABA: (*Angry*) Who is it that enters this Forest? Who is it that destroys my trees? I am the Guardian of this Forest. I say, "Death to the evil one!"

ENKIDU: Kill him, Gilgamesh! You don't know him like I do. Kill him!

HUMBABA: I see your weapons. They don't frighten me. I say, "Death to you!"

ELDER 4: The monster spit out flames of white fire. Fear shot into the heart of Gilgamesh. Stunned by the power of the beast, he could not attack!

HUMBABA: Ha! I thought so. You are weak. You cringe before me. Now, go!

ELDER 1: But not Enkidu! The demon Humbaba had stirred his blood red-hot.

ENKIDU: Praise and glory await you, Gilgamesh. Kill the monster—now!

ELDER 1: Humbaba roared. He skewed his face into a horrible grin and pawed the ground like an enraged bull. All weapons failed to harm him!

ELDER 5: The men were desperate! Gilgamesh cried out to the sun god for help.

ELDER 4: Protecting one of his own, the sun god sent down the Winds—a mad flurry that swept around Humbaba like sharp needles of burning glass.

HUMBABA: Please—please, Gilgamesh—and you, Enkidu, spare me! The god Enil made me Guardian of the Forest. I was only doing my job!

ENKIDU: Close your ears, Gilgamesh. He's evil. The monster must die!

ELDER 1: Enkidu drew his sword.

HUMBABA: No, Enkidu! Stop—or I *promise* you will die an early death!

ELDER 4: Gilgamesh hesitated no longer. His sword flashed in the sunlight.

ELDER 1: Then he smiled. His bright blade sang through the air, and with one slash, the hideous head of Humbaba fell off. (*Pause*) It was finished.

ELDER 5: (*Pause*) The two friends, finally victorious, started back to Uruk.

ELDER 4: But the fierce battle had left them dirty. Their tunics were stained and torn. So, pausing on their journey home, they washed away the blood and grime in a bubbling stream, refreshing their appearance.

ELDER 4: Now Gilgamesh looked resplendent again, shining, every inch a king.

ELDER 1: He was almost *too* successful, in this regard—almost too handsome, for on their way home, they met the goddess Ishtar.

ELDER 2: Oh! Is this when the goddess Ishtar falls in love with Gilgamesh?

ELDER 3: Well, I read that *he* was not interested in *her*. In fact, he *insulted* her.

ELDER 4: Not a good move. Rejected by the king, Ishtar became furious.

ELDER 1: She wanted revenge! She ran to her father, that same king of the gods, Anu, and insisted he send the Bull of Heaven down to Uruk. Anu gave in to Ishtar, but he feared the Bull meant disaster for the city.

ELDER 4: Anu was right. Snorting and bellowing, the Bull of Heaven ripped open great holes in the ground—earthquakes to swallow up hundreds of men. Lakes and rivers went dry. A terrible plague broke out.

ELDER 5: Obviously, something had to be done. The Bull had to be stopped.

ELDER 1: Stopped? Destroyed! This time, without help from the Winds or the gods, the two brothers killed the Bull of Heaven and saved the people.

ELDER 4: But all was not well, for soon after, Enkidu dreamed a terrible dream, a nightmare. Was his nightmare a horrible premonition?

ELDER 5: Indeed, the gods were in council, perturbed by these recent deaths. Humbaba of the Forest had been killed. Now, too, the Bull of Heaven. Punishment must be meted out. Who was the more responsible?

ANU: Gilgamesh—the king. He is responsible! (*Pause*) But must he die?

ELDER 4: The brothers cannot know the reasoning of the gods, cannot know their decision to spare the king. But if not the king, then *who*?

ELDER 5: Soon, it came to pass that Enkidu fell ill. For twelve days and twelve nights he suffered, growing weaker and weaker and weaker.

ELDER 1: Gilgamesh was distraught. Nothing made Enkidu well. The gods had sealed his fate. Finally, at dawn, on the thirteenth day, Enkidu died.

SOUND A: (*Chimes tinkle softly.*)

GILGAMESH: (*Slowly, softly*) Oh, Enkidu, Enkidu. This cannot be! I touch your heart, and I listen for your voice, but all is quiet. You are so still.

SOUNDS A,C: (*Chimes stop. Slow, low drumbeats during the next five speeches*)

ELDER 1: Gilgamesh offered prayers and sacrifices to honor Enkidu, but they did not soften the pain of losing his comrade, his friend, his brother.

ELDER 2: We know Enkidu was human. Being a man, he had to die. What about Gilgamesh—two-thirds god but one-third man. What about him?

ELDER 1: It was this very question that began to haunt Gilgamesh.

GILGAMESH: Must I, too, leave this earth? Must I die like Enkidu? No! I can't!

ELDER 1:	Then, in his pain, he remembered old Utnapishtim! (*Ut-na-pish'-tim*)
SOUND C:	(*Sharp thumps on drum, then silence*)
GILGAMESH:	He and his wife never die! They go on living forever. I must seek out Utnapishtim and learn his secret of eternal life!
ELDER 4:	Tightening his robes of sadness, Gilgamesh started on his lonely quest, seeking an old man who lives on the Waters of Death.
ELDER 5:	The difficult path led him across tall mountains and past two fierce Beings, The Twin Scorpions, who stopped Gilgamesh and questioned him over and over. Finally, they let him proceed.
ELDER 4:	At last he reached a ferry boat at the edge of the Waters of Death.
URSHANABI:	(*Ugly laugh*) Who goes there? Who seeks my ferry boat? Speak!
GILGAMESH:	It is I, King Gilgamesh. Ply your oars and take me to Utnapishtim!
URSHANABI:	(*Scornful laugh*) That old man? Little good that will do you, king!
GILGAMESH:	Urshanabi, take me across these Waters! (*Ur-shan-ah'-be*)
URSHANABI:	You may be the king, but I row only to the old man's island out there.
GILGAMESH:	If he is there, then shove off! Row, man, row! I must see Utnapishtim!
ELDER 3:	And when they reached Utnapishtim's island?
URSHANABI:	The old man you seek stands there, on the shore. I leave you now.
SOUND B:	(*Quiet piping that gradually fades away*)
UTNAPISHTIM:	So. And what do you want with me, Gilgamesh?

GILGAMESH: Please, I wish to learn the secret of life from you. I have lost my comrade in death. (*Pause*) Oh, Utnapishtim, I don't want to die!

UTNAPISHTIM: I see . . . but it is necessary, even helpful, to be sad and mournful when you lose someone you love and esteem. However, one must go on and make the best of his life. Man cannot conquer Death. This is his fate.

GILGAMESH: But *you* have eternal life. What is your secret? I beg you, tell me!

UTNAPISHTIM: It is not a secret. My gift came about long, long ago, at a time when the gods grew so angry with mankind that they wanted to rid the earth of all living beings.

GILGAMESH: But that didn't happen to you.

UTNAPISHTIM: No. One god told me to destroy my house and to build a large boat.

GILGAMESH: Did you do that—build a large boat?

UTNAPISHTIM: I did. The god had spoken. We built a boat big enough for my family, the craftsmen, and the animals. When we finished, the rains began.

GILGAMESH: The rains?

UTNAPISHTIM: Six days and six nights it rained. The waters rose higher and higher.

GILGAMESH: The land must have disappeared, even the mountains?

UTNAPISHTIM: So I feared. Thus, on the seventh day, I released a dove into the air to see if she could find land. But she came back. No land. No trees.

GILGAMESH: You must have tried again. Maybe you sent out other birds?

UTNAPISHTIM: I sent out a swallow, but she came back, too. Then I sent a raven, who didn't come back.

GILGAMESH: The raven found land? You must have saved all the people then.

UTNAPISHTIM: No, I didn't. When I looked for the people, they all had turned to clay. Only my wife and I were left, but we weren't supposed to be alive. Some of the gods were angry with each other—and with us.

GILGAMESH: Yet you survived—you and your wife. How come?

UTNAPISHTIM: The gods couldn't blame us for surviving, so they made a peaceful agreement among themselves. Then they gave us our endless lives.

GILGAMESH: Oh, Utnapishtim, how I long to have a life without death!

UTNAPISHTIM: But is an eternal life truly your destiny?

GILGAMESH: My destiny? Of course! Please, just tell me what to do.

UTNAPISHTIM: Well, there is a test. (*Pause*) The test is difficult: You must not sleep for seven nights and six days.

GILGAMESH: Stay awake that long? I can easily do that!

ELDER 1: But King Gilgamesh couldn't stay awake. He failed his test. So Utnapishtim, tired of the king's useless begging, sent him away.

ELDER 4: Then, thanks to the mercy of Utnapishtim's wife, Gilgamesh learned of a magic plant. When it's swallowed, it makes old men young!

ELDER 5: Miraculously, Gilgamesh found the plant! Planning to use it later, when he grew old, he tucked the plant away and started back to Uruk.

ELDER 1: Unfortunately, he stopped to bathe in a lake, and he set the plant aside for safekeeping, on the shore. But something happened!

ELDER 4: A snake, fascinated by this new plant, stole it—and swallowed it.

GILGAMESH: Horrified, I watched the snake slither along—then stop. Then it began—*to shed its skin!*

ELDER 1: In a moment, the snake emerged with a new skin.

GILGAMESH: The snake . . . the snake was young again!

ELDER 4: All his hopes for a long, youthful life had disappeared into that snake.

GILGAMESH: My quest was finished. My search for youth and for eternal life had failed.

SOUND C: (*Muffled drumming*)

GILGAMESH: That evening, I stood on the mountaintop and marveled at my city. Sturdy walls enclosed the life I'd left. I had built those walls. I had kept my people safe—but I could do more. As the sun dipped in the west, I walked on, through the city gates and into the heart of the city.

ELDER 2: Has nothing come from this experience for Gilgamesh?

GILGAMESH: The moon rose. Stars began to shine, and my spirits rose. I felt now I could push Death out of my mind and go on, to live life to its fullest.

ELDER 3: Oh, good! Do you think he ever fulfilled his destiny as king?

ELDER 1: Certainly, my friend. We have twelve clay tablets to prove that he did. Remember, *Gilgamesh*, from pre-Iraqi days, is an Arabian myth of epic proportions!

SOUNDS A, B, C: (*Muffled drumming fades, whistle chirps, chimes tinkle; all fade out.*)

Myths from Around the World: Greece

Hercules and the Watchdog of Hades

INTRODUCTION

Today we need a hero, an extraordinary person—someone larger than life—someone like the powerful, mythical Hercules. After all, he is godlike, but he is human, and although all his Labors are fantastic adventures, they are not just wild adventures. They are serious punishments that hold both drama and sentiment for us.

The auspicious life of Hercules begins when Zeus, the all-powerful Greek god, plans to create a powerful and wise son, one who will be able to protect both gods and humans against disaster. To assure that he will produce such a special son, Zeus chooses a wise and beautiful woman, Alcmene, to be the child's mother. When Hercules is born of this union, unfortunately, trouble begins.

Zeus's wife, the goddess Hera, rages with jealousy and anger. She vows to get rid of this child. First she sends two serpents to kill him, but Hercules strangles them with his bare hands. Later, when he is grown, she casts a mad fit upon him, which causes him to go berserk, attack his friends, and kill his family. He finally emerges from Hera's spell and is distraught at the horror he has caused.

Anxious to redeem himself, Hercules seeks advice from the famed oracle at Delphi, who sends him to King Eurystheus for his punishment. The king assigns him Twelve Labors. The last Labor, and perhaps the most dangerous, requires Hercules to conquer the three-headed ravenous dog Cerberus, which guards the gates of Hades.

Poets and artists throughout the centuries have drawn inspiration from the story of Hercules, who conquers the watchdog Cerberus with only his wits and his prodigious strength.

PRODUCTION NOTES

Many myths from Greece and around the world try to describe the mysterious, unknown land of the dead. In the following script about Hercules and his journey to Hades, we are introduced to one boundary, the River Styx; the ferry boatman Charon; and, above all, the fierce dog who guards the gates of Hades, keeping the living out and the dead within. The Twelfth Labor of Hercules, mythical and impossible, highlights this Greek hero's physical abilities and his determination to personally atone for the horrific crimes he committed.

A minimum of twelve scripts will be needed, including one for the teacher. The exact number will depend on the number of Heroes chosen for the chorus. At least two students, and as many as five or six, can be Heroes. This group provides commentary on the action and makes noises that almost act as sound effects. The heroic work of this group will surely bring excitement to the script.

Explorers 1 and 2 act as knowledgeable guides for the inquisitive Student.

The Student is always questioning and responding, often in a brash way.

Narrators 1–6 keep the thread of the story moving.

Hercules and the Watchdog of Hades

Hercules and the Watchdog of Hades

A Greek Myth

```
                          Heroes
                        X X X X X

Narrators 3, 2, 1                          Narrators 4, 5, 6
   X X X                                       X X X

            Explorer 1     Student     Explorer 2
                X             X             X
```

EXPLORER 1: Hey! Hello, out there! We're looking for a hero—somebody special—somebody outstanding—a hero!

HEROES: (*Beat on chests*) Heroes! Heroes! Look! Here!

EXPLORER 2: I don't think so. No offense, guys, but we're looking for an *extra* ordinary man—a man of know-how, courage, and great strength.

HEROES: Here! Here! Over here!

EXPLORER 1: Sorry. We're in Ancient Greece, and we need a really *big* man, one larger than life—a Greek hero!

HEROES: (*Sadly, softly*) Ohhhh.

STUDENT: Too bad. That leaves you out. (*Pause*) I could offer you my services.

HEROES: (*Laughter*)

From *More Readers Theatre for Middle School Boys: Adventures with Mythical Creatures* by Ann N. Black. Santa Barbara, CA: Teacher Ideas Press/Libraries Unlimited. Copyright © 2009.

NARRATOR 1: Sorry. We're moving on to Hades. The three-headed dog is waiting there—not to mention Herakles. (*Hair'-a-kleez*)

EXPLORER 2: Oh, good choice for a hero—Herakles!

STUDENT: Excuse me, don't you mean *Hercules?* (*Herk'-u-leez*)

NARRATOR 3: No. Herakles—that's his Greek name. What you know is the Roman name. That came later.

STUDENT: Well, it's *Hercules* in my dictionary.

EXPLORER 1: Okay, I guess we can go with Hercules.

HEROES: Whew!

STUDENT: Wait. You mentioned a "three-headed dog," right along with that Herakles name. That makes me think.

HEROES: (*Short burst of scoffing laughter*)

STUDENT: Not funny! Are we talking about a real man-hero or one of those Greek-god heroes who just happens to have a dog?

NARRATOR 2: Ah, the dog comes later. As for Hercules—well, some say he was human. Some say he was a god, or at least that he *became* a god.

NARRATOR 1: To begin, the most powerful of all the gods, Zeus, was the father of Hercules. But his mother was not the goddess Hera, the wife of Zeus.

STUDENT: Uh-oh. The plot thickens—a jealous stepmother, right?

NARRATOR 4: Yes, but you see, Zeus had a noble purpose. He wanted a son who would be wise and powerful, who could protect both gods and men.

NARRATOR 6: So Zeus chose a wise and beautiful woman, Alcmene. (*Alk-mee'-na*)

NARRATOR 5: Zeus did name their son after his wife, Hera—you know, Herakles.

STUDENT: Somehow, I don't think that would please her a whole lot.

NARRATOR 1: Uh . . . no. Hera set out to destroy Hercules on Day One.

NARRATOR 4: In fact, when Hercules was only a baby, she sent him a deadly gift—two serpents, designed to get rid of him.

HEROES: (*Slow hissing begins.*)

NARRATOR 5: (*Slow, low, mysterious*) Was it the sound—or his instinct? Hercules woke up. He didn't scream. He didn't cry out. But there, in the soft moonlight, he saw them. Every muscle in his young body grew tight.

NARRATOR 6: Two serpents, glowing green and mystical, were dangling above his bed, twisting and turning. Long, black tongues slowly slid in and out, in and out. Four tiny eyes bulged, crazy with hunger. Rotten fangs, crusted with venom, snapped up and down, up and down.

NARRATOR 1: Strings of something sticky and yellow dripped on his skin. Then, suddenly, Hercules was choking! The air . . . the air was poisonous!

HEROES: (*Hissing grows louder.*)

NARRATOR 2: He gasped for air, but he waited. (*Pause*) Silently, the serpents slithered down, into his cradle. They arched, ready to strike!

NARRATOR 3: Hercules reached out. He caught hold of the writhing, slippery bodies. Then, with his bare hands, he twisted once, and twisted again!

HEROES: (*Hissing stops.*)

NARRATOR 4: Only an infant, Hercules had strangled two huge serpents.

STUDENT: Excuse me—we are into a myth, aren't we? Was that for real?

EXPLORER 2: Got the picture, huh? Well, you haven't heard the half of it!

NARRATOR 1: Later, when Hercules was a young man, married and with children, Hera, still breathing revenge, cast a spell over him—a fit of madness that made Hercules attack his friends, even kill his wife and children.

HEROES: Wooooo. Maad!

STUDENT: Mad and crazy-creepy!

NARRATOR 5: But he finally recovers his senses. Then he realizes what he's done.

NARRATOR 6: But what can he do to make up for all the pain, the blood, the deaths?

NARRATOR 1: He must visit Delphi. The wise oracle at Delphi can advise him.

HEROES: (*Whispers*) Eurystheus. Eurystheus. Eurystheus! (*Your-is'-thee-us*)

EXPLORER 1: The oracle decrees that King Eurystheus will decide his punishment.

EXPLORER 2: And the king's sentence is twelve impossible tasks. Twelve Labors!

STUDENT: Is Hera behind this, too? Is she in cahoots with that king, Eurystheus?

EXPLORER 1: You'd better believe it!

EXPLORER 2: But remember, he does get a little help from his friends—some of the friendly gods, especially from the goddess Athene.

EXPLORER 1: Luckily. So, thanks to them, he starts out with a sword, a bow and arrows, a golden breastplate, and a special robe from Athene.

NARRATOR 4: His First Labor: go to nearby Numea. A ferocious, man-eating lion is attacking and killing everyone there. His mission: destroy that lion!

NARRATOR 1: He tracks the lion, all right, and he tries to kill it, but he can't! His weapons are useless! They're made of the finest iron and bronze, yet they can't even pierce the lion's skin.

NARRATOR 5: They're useless! He must have a weapon made of wood.

NARRATOR 6: So Hercules cuts down an olive tree and makes a huge, wooden club.

NARRATOR 1: Armed with the wooden weapon, Hercules again approaches the lion.

NARRATOR 2: But the lion is unafraid. It doesn't move. It just lies there. Hercules raises his club—and he swings, hitting the lion and stunning it. (*Pause*) The lion stirs. Hercules beats it—beats it back down again

HEROES: Pow! Pow!

NARRATOR 3: Then, with only his hands, Hercules strangles the deadly lion.

NARRATOR 4: And, using the lion's own claws, he strips off the magic skin, and throws it around his shoulders. Now *he's* protected against all fine weapons of iron and bronze. *He's* invulnerable!

HEROES: Yaay! (*Clapping*)

STUDENT: So, one Labor down. Eleven to go. (*Pause*) Time for the dog story?

EXPLORER 1: No. Not yet. Not yet! Be patient.

EXPLORER 2: Hercules must kill the Hydra—a slimy thing that lives in a black, fetid swamp—a water monster with nine snaky heads, the Hydra, a monster who smelled of stagnant water and something soft and rotten.

EXPLORER 1: Besides the awful, foul odor of her skin, her breath was so putrid, so disgusting, it could kill you, just like that!

EXPLORER 2: Death. When any of her snake heads opened its mouth—death!

STUDENT: No! Talk about bad breath! Run away! Run away! Run away!

NARRATOR 1: Hardly. Hercules finds the monster and stands before her. One head lunges toward him, its eyes flashing, its mouth open—breathing!

NARRATOR 4: Hercules gags and chokes. He's suffocating! (*Pause*) But no, he picks up his club and smacks the snake head again and again, until the eyes grow dim, the breathing stops, and finally, until nothing's left.

NARRATOR 5: Nothing but a stinkpot of rotting gore. Hercules takes a deep breath.

HEROES: (*Take a big breath; exhale*)

NARRATOR 3: But, look! That black muck is twitching. The dead Hydra is heaving—it's growing! It's another snake head!

NARRATOR 2: The Hydra laughs a loud, shrill, fiendish cry.

NARRATOR 1: Hercules draws his sword this time, and with one sharp slice, he cuts off the Hydra's main head.

HEROES: Yaaay!

NARRATOR 2: (*Slowly, sternly*) No more laughter now.

NARRATOR 3: Hercules cuts up the dead body and dips his arrows into the last of the Hydra—a cesspool of black, poisonous gall bubbling at his feet.

HEROES: Oh, yuck!

STUDENT: Wow! That was great! What's next?

NARRATOR 4: For his Third Labor, Hercules had to capture a beautiful, red deer, but she escaped him for a whole year before he caught her.

NARRATOR 5: After that, he had to capture a huge, rampaging, bellowing boar.

NARRATOR 6: Hercules trapped this swine in a huge snowbank, bound it with chains, threw it across his shoulders, and carried it to King Eurystheus.

STUDENT: Okay, I'm impressed. Is it time for the dog story yet?

EXPLORER 1: Patience. Patience! A major clean-up job's ahead!

EXPLORER 2: Hercules has to clean up the mess made by three thousand oxen. No one has cleaned out their Augean (*Aw'-gee-un*) stables in thirty years.

HEROES: Euwwww!

EXPLORER 1: Imagine that smell! Then think about cleaning out those stables.

EXPLORER 2: And to clean up those stockyards—in one day!

NARRATOR 4: Hercules performs this task—his Fifth Labor—with two rivers, forcing them to flow right through the stockyards, then through the stables. The rivers clean everything and wash the whole mess out to the sea!

HEROES: (*Clapping*)

STUDENT: What's next? He's almost halfway through the Twelve Labors.

EXPLORER 1: He has to kill a huge flock of birds. They're fiendish! They're roosting high up in the trees, and every day they send down foul, black droppings on everyone nearby.

EXPLORER 2: Then they shoot out their bronze feathers, killing, killing, killing.

HEROES:	Euwwww!
NARRATOR 1:	The birds won't leave the trees. Consequently, the arrows of Hercules are useless—until Athene sends down huge, bronze castanets. Hercules bangs the heavy metal, and the noise scares the birds out of the trees!
NARRATOR 2:	Taking careful aim, he shoots! His poison arrows destroy every bird.
EXPLORER 1:	Now we're up to the Seventh Labor, when Hercules captures a wild bull that belches fire. He takes this beast, still alive, to Eurystheus.
NARRATOR 1:	But with no thanks! On to task Eight:
	to capture four savage horses that eat no grain. Their owner feeds these mares only human flesh.
HEROES:	(*Disgustedly*) Euwww!
NARRATOR 4:	Hercules kills the owner, tames the mares, and takes them to the king.
HEROES:	All right!
STUDENT:	Hey. You *promised* the dog story. A three-headed dog can't be any worse than people-eating mares. That was totally gross!
EXPLORER 1:	Well, you're right. We did promise.
EXPLORER 2:	Okay. We'll skip the Amazons, the red cattle, and the golden apples.
STUDENT:	For real? We're moving on? (*Pause*) Bring on the Twelfth Labor!
HEROES:	(*Clapping*)
EXPLORER 1:	Well, prepare yourself. It's on to Hades, the Underworld!
STUDENT:	So what's so spooky? The Underworld is not real.
NARRATOR 1:	Not real? Really? Hmm. So *you* say!

EXPLORER 1: Well, here's the situation. Zeus was king of everything *on* Earth. His brother, the god Poseidon, was lord of all the waters.

EXPLORER 2: And the third brother, Hades, ruled everything *under* the earth—every body—basically, all the ghosts of the dead.

EXPLORER 1: Ghosts, okay—or you can call them spirits, or shades.

HEROES: Cool! Cool! Ghoul!

EXPLORER 1: Not so fast, guys. It wasn't easy to get to the Underworld, especially if you were a living person. Then, if and when you finally reached the Gates of Hades, there was Cerberus, the watchdog of Hades, chained there to keep out all the living people and to keep in all the ghosts.

STUDENT: At last—the dog! This myth is really coming alive. Scared? No way!

HEROES: (*Ominously*) Wait. Alive? (*Low, ominous laughter*)

NARRATOR 4: So Hercules journeys to the land of the dead, where he must capture the watchdog of Hades alive, then bring the dog to Eurystheus.

NARRATOR 4: Right. Hercules leaves the safety of his home and travels east and north, until he reaches the thick, churning waters of the Black Sea.

HEROES: Go! Go!

NARRATOR 5: Here he finds the first river that will lead him to the land of the dead—the Acheron. (*Ak'-er-on*)

NARRATOR 6: He steps into the black waters. They seem quiet, serene. (*Slowly becomes excited*) Then he feels the waves begin to rise.

NARRATOR 5: The waters swell. They become noisy and turbulent! Then, suddenly, all is quiet again. A sluggish stream lies before him. It's the boundary of the Underworld, the River Styx, the river he must cross. (*Sticks*)

NARRATOR 3: Hercules rubs his eyes, trying to see this place. Ahead of him, thin, pale ghosts hover on the shore. And there's the ferryboat, and that ugly, twisted creature must be Charon, the ferryboatman. (*Kaa'-ron*)

NARRATOR 2: The ferryboatman jerks his head and holds out his hand for payment. Hercules presses two gold coins into the scabby hand, and he steps into the leaky boat. It rocks and dips and begins to move.

NARRATOR 3: Hercules can feel the presence of Athene. Yet, for the first time, his blood runs cold with fear.

NARRATOR 1: The dead smell of rotting garbage and slick muck envelopes him like a shroud of death. He shakes his head. He must be clear, be ready!

NARRATOR 4: The boat docks, and the air *explodes* with the wild barking of dogs. But, no. (*Pause*) Not dogs—*one* dog—one enormous dog with three gigantic heads.

NARRATOR 3: It's Cerberus, spitting and howling from three furious throats.

NARRATOR 5: Hercules steps from the boat. He walks slowly toward the dog. Filthy, matted fur heaves and creeps along the dog's bony back. Eyes from every head spew pus and hate and anger.

NARRATOR 6: Hercules raises his hand. At once, three jaws open—wide. Nine tails twitch and whip. But they're not tails at all—they're snakes!

HEROES: (*Short blast of loud hissing*)

NARRATOR 5: One jerks. It strikes. It aims for Hercules, goes for his hand, his arm!

NARRATOR 4: (*Intensely*) But the lion's skin is protecting him! Fearless now, Hercules grabs one thick neck and presses against the throat with all his strength. The throat gurgles. Eyeballs bulge and bleed. The head is weakening. The jaws fall open. Yellow teeth snap. This is it!

75

NARRATOR 1: But Hercules is fighting for his own breath. His muscles ripple in the gray-white light of the Underworld. Then, with a hoarse cry from his own throat, he twists the neck, and it snaps like a worm-infested log.

NARRATOR 4: He presses on the next throat, and the dog snarls and spits in anger. Nine razor-sharp tails thrash and whine in the air. Hercules presses harder. The second head snaps—then the third. Sticky, white froth bubbles slowly from the muzzles of the three silent heads.

NARRATOR 1: The tails drop. The once violent beast is helpless. Hercules binds the limp body with strong, heavy metal chains. Cerberus is still alive, and now he must drag it all the way back to Eurystheus.

HEROES: (*Loud whisper*) Eurystheus! Eurystheus. Eurystheus.

EXPLORER 2: Up to King Eurystheus, then back to the Gates of Hades again.

STUDENT: Back? He returns the dog? It's still there?

NARRATOR 1: So they say.

STUDENT: Really? Well, what happens to Hercules? Are his Labors finished?

NARRATOR 4: They are. He has satisfied his obligations and redeemed himself.

STUDENT: Good. Does Hera finally stop picking on him?

EXPLORER 2: Well, you know, that's another story—or two.

STUDENT: Oh, come on!

HEROES: Aha!

EXPLORER 1: But you get the picture, right? Hercules—our Greek hero, an extraordinary man, larger than life!

HEROES: (*Beating on chests again*) Heroes! Heroes! Heroes!

Myths from Around the World: Greece

Searching for Snakes

INTRODUCTION

Much of our English literary heritage is indebted to the rich imaginations of the ancient Greeks. Their extraordinary stories, their fundamental moralities, and their connections with real life combine in a plethora of oral and written literature. Stories of gods and goddesses, jealousy and temptation, anger and compassion, and monsters and miracles continue to amaze and thrill us after eight thousand years.

Several Greek myths revolve around the mystique of Medusa, the Gorgon monster, who is described by *The Oxford Classical Dictionary* as having "a round, ugly face, snakes instead of hair, a belt of the teeth of a boar, sometimes a beard, huge wings, and eyes that could transform people into stone." Above all, she is a symbol of unremitting power, and it's her demise that propels this story and succeeding myths.

This myth actually begins with King Acrisius, who is afraid of dying. When an oracle predicts that his future grandson will cause his death, the old king imprisons his only daughter, Danae, in a tower to isolate her from all human contact. However, the god Zeus falls in love with the beautiful Danae, and using his powers, he appears before her in a shower of gold. Soon after this visit, the ill-fated grandson, the demigod Perseus, is born.

The journey Perseus undertakes years later to save his mother not only destroys the evil Medusa, but also establishes the transfer of her power to others.

The Medusa myth is as exciting and rewarding today as it must have been in ancient Greece, for it incorporates both the fears and aspirations of human beings and their counterparts, the mythical gods and goddesses on Mount Olympus.

PRODUCTION NOTES

Visual aspects of the Medusa myth have intrigued artists for centuries. In words, clay, and paint, authors and artists have tried to express the horror of this monster. Today students, too, may be intrigued to use their artistic talents to describe the characters and events of this myth. Gods and goddesses and ancient magic are all dramatic subjects, but best of all might be Medusa, with her bulging eyes and wild head crawling with snakes.

The following script calls for a cast of approximately fourteen—approximately, as the chorus of Heroes can vary in size from two to as many as seven or eight. Basically, fifteen scripts will be needed, including one for the teacher.

The chorus of Heroes speaks in response to the actions and words of the other characters. They should respond enthusiastically, but not boisterously.

Narrators 1–6 are inside the story. They set up the background of the myth, understand the problems the characters face, and maintain the narrative flow.

Explorers 1 and 2, savvy about ancient Greece and its myths, bring the readers and the audience into their adventure. The Explorers are guides for the Student, and for us.

The Student is questioning and unknowing. He represents any listener about to be immersed in a strange world.

NOTE: A small pile or a row of stones arranged on the stage before the performance begins is apt to provoke a welcome note of curiosity about this myth.

Searching for Snakes

Searching for Snakes

The Medusa Myth

```
                        Heroes
                      X X X X X

  Narrators 3, 2, 1                         Narrators 4, 5, 6
      X X X                                     X X X

          Explorer 1     Student     Explorer 2
              X             X             X
```

EXPLORER 1: Hey! Watch what you're doing there! Don't you see those stones?

STUDENT: Sure. So what? What do a bunch of stones have to do with our adventure? You *said* we'd have an adventure.

EXPLORER 2: We will. We will! But the stones first. (*Pause*) They may be people.

HEROES: (*Quietly laughing among themselves at this ridiculous idea*)

STUDENT: Hey, I'm with them! It's a joke, right?

EXPLORER 1: Ah, maybe. But they *might* be people—dead people—dead people from Greece, Ancient Greece—like in this adventure.

EXPLORER 2: I don't think this guy is ready—not for *this* adventure. It's too wild.

STUDENT:	Hey—try me!
EXPLORER 1:	Well, if you promise to stick close to us, and to treat those stones with care, I guess we can take a chance on you.
HEROES:	Yaaay!
EXPLORER 2:	That's settled then. We're off to Greece—old, *old* Greece.
STUDENT:	Hold on! I can't speak Greek, much less read Greek!
EXPLORER 1:	No matter—we're plunging into one of their myths.
STUDENT:	I *have* read some of those, especially the scary ones. I like them best.
EXPLORER 1:	(*Exaggerating*) Oh, you mean when heads get chopped off, and black blood spills out; when people turn into fire-breathing animals, and ghosts visit your dreams.
HEROES:	(*Scared*) Wooooo.
EXPLORER 2:	Ghosts—dead people only half-buried, who might *need* you.
EXPLORER 1:	Oh, you like those scary myths when big snakes hiss, and monsters seize you by the throat and shake your heart out!
STUDENT:	Yes! Yes, that's the kind!
HEROES:	(*Silent*)
EXPLORER 1:	Right, then let's begin with Zeus. He's the main Greek god.
HEROES:	Zeussss. Zeussss. Zeus!
NARRATOR 1:	Zeus—the leader, the ruler of everything on earth, and like all the gods, he would never die. He is immortal, powerful, and wise.
NARRATOR 3:	Well, he was wise, *most* of the time.

NARRATOR 2: Right—*most* of the time—except for the beautiful women.

NARRATOR 4: He often fell in love, not with just a goddess, but with a real woman on Earth. But when he visited her, he never appeared as a god.

NARRATOR 5: Oh, no. He was ingenious. He could change his shape. One time he left Mount Olympus and appeared on Earth as a swan.

STUDENT: You're kidding me! A swan?

EXPLORER 1: Hey! Be cool! We're trying to get the facts here—the mythical facts.

EXPLORER 2: So, we begin with Zeus up on Mount Olympus, a beautiful young woman on Earth, and her father, King Acrisius. (*Ah-cree'-see-us*)

STUDENT: Uh-oh. That doesn't sound good!

NARRATOR 6: That's an understatement! The king is nervous and upset.

NARRATOR 4: Old King Acrisius is afraid of dying. He asks himself, "When will this happen? Why? How can I prevent this—dying?" Desperate, he travels to the mountains to consult a wise man, an oracle, for advice.

NARRATOR 5: When he arrives at the mystical mountain valley, he sees steam rising from a jagged crater in the ground. This is it—the home of the oracle!

HEROES: (*Sounds of steam punctuate the next two speeches.*)

NARRATOR 6: Barely breathing, King Acrisius draws a packet of herbs from his cloak. The oracle is about to make himself known. Hurry!

NARRATOR 4: The steam twists and knots, drawing the king closer and closer to the crater. He begins to tremble. He tears open the little packet of herbs, and with a hoarse cry, flings the fragrant seeds into the steam.

HEROES:	(*Steam grows stronger.*)
NARRATOR 6:	The steam flares! A voice emerges, like something from the grave!
NARRATOR 3:	"Down!" the voice cries. "Down on the ground, oh, king!"
NARRATOR 6:	It's the oracle! He has spoken—given the king orders! The old king gathers his rich robes about him and throws himself to the ground.
HEROES:	(*Steam stops.*)
NARRATOR 5:	(*Loud whispering from king*) "Oh, mighty oracle," he says, "speak to me! Tell me about the future! I don't want to die! What shall I do?"
NARRATOR 6:	The steam bubbles and drifts. No longer pale and transparent, reds and purples hover above the king. And the voice speaks again:
NARRATOR 3:	"Ah, King Acrisius. Fear not. Your life spins forth like a mighty river, flowing on and on. Rejoice! Rejoice—*until* you have a grandson."
NARRATOR 6:	Then the ground moves. It shakes violently. It shudders and groans! Panic grips the old king. He cries out to the oracle.
NARRATOR 5:	"Grandson? No! I have only one daughter, my beautiful Danae! A grandson? No!" (*Dan'-eye*)
NARRATOR 3:	"The fates do not lie. If your daughter gives you a grandson, he will cause your death. Now, go. Eat ten grains of herbs and return home."
NARRATOR 6:	Tears stream down the old king's face. How can he prevent this?
NARRATOR 5:	"What can I do? No! I can't kill my only daughter! No, oracle, no!"

NARRATOR 6: But the steam fades away—only the wind rushes to the old man's ears. Finally, slowly, he counts out the ten grains of herbs. Then, chewing the bitter weeds, he makes his way home—thinking, thinking.

NARRATOR 4: Then he has it! Seated on his throne again, he issues a royal order.

HEROES: (*Two claps*)

NARRATOR 5: "Go! Find my daughter," he says. "Lock her up in the tower. She shall have no more visitors on this earth from now on!"

HEROES: (*Three claps*)

NARRATOR 1: Meanwhile, up on Mount Olympus, the god Zeus is restless. He looks down upon the earth and spies the beautiful young woman—Danae, the only daughter of King Acrisius. Now *Zeus* has an idea.

STUDENT: Wait—that beautiful young woman, Danae, is locked up in a tower!

NARRATOR 1: Not a problem for Zeus! He appears to her in a shower of gold.

STUDENT: A shower of gold? Oh, sure.

EXPLORER 1: Yes! Now, you can probably guess what happens next.

HEROES: Per-see-us. Per-see-us. Perseus! (*Per'-see-us*)

EXPLORER 2: Yep! Our hero is born—our hero, the young half-god Perseus.

EXPLORER 2: The news travels fast to the king. He is stunned and frightened.

NARRATOR 5: "Grandson!" he cries. "Grandson? How can that be! Take them away, away, do you hear? Lock them up tight in some old wood chest and cast them into the sea!"

STUDENT: Wow. And that's the end of the adventure?

EXPLORER 1: Nope. That's the *beginning* of this adventure.

NARRATOR 1: So, part of the fortune-telling has come true.

HEROES: Part? *Part*?

EXPLORER 2: Oh, this is good—very good. The plot's getting tough.

STUDENT: But are they rescued from the sea? They have to be rescued.

NARRATOR 2: Yes. Their wooden chest drifts to another Greek island, where they *are* rescued and protected by King Polydcctcs. (*Poll-ee-dek'-teez*)

HEROES: (*Brief clapping of hands*) Yes. Yes!

NARRATOR 3: Years pass, and Perseus grows into a strong young man, but trouble lies ahead for his mother, the still beautiful Danae. Look to the king!

NARRATOR 2: King Polydectes has fallen in love with her. But *she* doesn't love him, and she certainly doesn't want to marry him.

NARRATOR 1: Of course Perseus takes his mother's side—which, of course, does not please Polydectes. Definitely not! Decision time again!

NARRATOR 2: He has to get rid of Perseus! But how? So the king begins to scheme.

HEROES: Uh-oh.

NARRATOR 3: He invites all the men on the island, including Perseus, to a rich feast.

NARRATOR 4: "To assure your allegiance to me," he announces, "I, King Polydectes, request the gift of a fine horse, in tribute to our throne."

NARRATOR 1: Perseus grows pale. "But, sire," he responds, "I have no horse to give."

NARRATOR 4: "What a pity," the king says. "If you had, I might have forsworn my marriage plans with our beautiful Danae."

NARRATOR 1: (*Angrily*) "King Polydectes," Perseus objects, "I could bring you the head of the Gorgon Medusa, easier than bring you a horse!" (*Meh-doo'-sa*)

HEROES: Uh-oh. Trouble. Trouble.

NARRATOR 4: The king laughs. "An excellent idea, Perseus. You will cut off Medusa's head and bring it to me? Good! Good! Go! Do it!"

NARRATOR 5: The king rubs his hands together. His scheme is working!

NARRATOR 4: Slyly, he speaks quietly to himself: "Go—and good riddance! Danae will marry me after all, for the Gorgons will destroy Perseus!"

STUDENT: What's so horrible about a Gorgon? I don't get it. What *is* a Gorgon?

EXPLORER 2: The Gorgons were three fierce monsters with huge, hideous heads, black teeth, tongues that lolled, and eyes that burned and stared. Worse, Medusa had long, wriggly snakes on her head instead of hair.

STUDENT: Oh, yuck!

HEROES: Uh-oh. Trouble. Trouble.

NARRATOR 1: But of the three Gorgons, Medusa was the only one that might be human.

STUDENT: Medusa? I thought a Medusa was that jellyfish with long tentacles.

NARRATOR 1: Not this Medusa. This is the original—the real thing.

EXPLORER 1: So Perseus starts on his journey to find the Medusa, unaware of the dangers that lie ahead of him.

NARRATOR 4: Luckily, the goddess Athene knows what's happening. To warn him, she describes the threats he will face and the steps he must follow on his mission. (*Ah-thee'-nah*)

NARRATOR 3: "Listen closely," she tells him. "Never, never look into the eyes of Medusa. If you do, she will act at once and turn you into stone!"

STUDENT: Stone—oh, like those—over there. (*Pause*) I see—I think.

NARRATOR 3: "Now," she continues, "first, you must find the nymphs. They will arm you further and give you directions to the three Gorgons. Once you find these monsters, do not mistake Medusa for the other two."

STUDENT: (*Whispers*) How can he cut off her head without looking at her?

EXPLORER 2: Sh. There's more.

NARRATOR 3: "Listen closely," she says, "and I will describe Medusa for you."

EXPLORER 2: Then Athene whispers in his ear, and Perseus grows amazed.

NARRATOR 3: "Now," she says, "I give you this gold-bright shield. When you find Medusa, look at her *reflection* in the shield—only her reflection."

STUDENT: Oh, that's clever! What else?

EXPLORER 1: Well, of course, he has to have a weapon. Very important.

STUDENT: Oh, yeah. You mean to . . . cut . . . cut off the head?

NARRATOR 4: Correct. Luckily, the god Hermes steps up for that with a sharp sword that he presents to the young man. (*Her'- meez*)

EXPLORER 2: He tells Perseus, "Guard it well, and the sword will serve you well."

STUDENT: Is he ready now?

EXPLORER 1: No. The goddess Athene, who watches over him, says he must first find the nymphs who have even more gifts for him.

NARRATOR 1: But where the nymphs live is a secret, and only three gray-haired old goddesses know that secret. So Perseus must begin with them.

NARRATOR 6: The three old goddesses have only one tooth and one eye among them, but they have three bad natures. One laughs a mean laugh and says, "Help you?" (*Laughs*) "No, we will never help you!"

NARRATOR 2: But Perseus *has* to find those nymphs.

NARRATOR 1: When nighttime comes (*Slowly, secretly*), he creeps up on the old goddesses, and he steals their one eye and their one tooth.

NARRATOR 6: Well, the old things go crazy! "Give those back," they cry. "That's all we have—one eye and one tooth! Give those back!"

NARRATOR 4: "Not until you tell me!" Perseus answers. "Where do the nymphs live? Tell me! I have to find out."

NARRATOR 5: "No! Never," they cry, but as the day wears on, the blind, toothless old crones give in and tell him where the nymphs live. Perseus wins!

NARRATOR 4: Using this secret knowledge, Perseus finds the nymphs, and they give him winged sandals to speed him through the air, a helmet that makes him invisible, and a leather bag to hold Medusa's head.

STUDENT: Oh, yuck!

NARRATOR 4: Of course! The gods think of everything! Now, fully armed, he can fly to another land—the land where the Gorgons live.

EXPLORER 1: This land is covered with stones—stones of all sizes and shapes, some like petrified bodies, dull and twisted by the eternal rains and wind.

EXPLORER 2: Perseus, invisible now, walks slowly and carefully among the stones. Then he sees two Gorgons—two monstrous creatures that stare wildly at the sound of his footsteps. But they're not what he's seeking—the dreaded Medusa.

EXPLORER 1: Then, all at once, he sees her, sitting beneath a gnarled, old tree. She's asleep.

EXPLORER 1: The air is silent. Nothing moves, except a twisted mass of snakes on Medusa's head. They seem to be in her hair—no! They *are* her hair.

EXPLORER 2: (*Gruesomely*) The snakes curl and squirm in long, greasy tendrils. Perseus takes a step forward. The snakes grow agitated, frantic. Slippery sounds hiss and spill as the black, barbed tongues dart in and out, back and forth.

HEROES: (*Agitated snake hissing*)

EXPLORER 1: Perseus draws his sword and takes another step. (*Pause*) The Medusa has not stirred. (*Pause*) He moves closer.

NARRATOR 3: "Do not look into her eyes," Athene had said.

EXPLORER 2: (*Slowly*) He takes a deep breath and raises the shining shield. He waits for the reflection of Medusa's head. (*Pause*) There! There it is!

EXPLORER 1: He takes one more, stealthy step. Now! He's standing before Medusa!

EXPLORER 2: His sword feels heavy in his hand. His brow is wet with sweat. Then, gradually, he begins to sense that Athene is guiding him. Courage!

NARRATOR 1: Now! With a mighty effort, Perseus swings his sword through the air.

EXPLORER 1: One blow—one swift cut—and Medusa's head falls to the ground.

HEROES: Yaaay!

EXPLORER 2: But Perseus is dumbfounded! Before him stands a winged horse, Pegasus, sprung alive from Medusa's blood and dead body!

EXPLORER 1: Ah, but Perseus is finished here. He puts the massive, slippery head of Medusa into the leather bag, and with his winged sandals, Perseus flies back to confront King Polydectes.

89

NARRATOR 4: Time has passed, but Perseus discovers immediately that the king is still determined to marry his mother, Danae.

NARRATOR 6: Desperate to save her from this fate, Perseus reaches into the leather bag. He grabs the still-pulsating head and shakes loose the wiry, slimy lump of snakes. Then he holds up the Medusa head and turns her blank, bulging eyes toward Polydectes and his court. Astonished, they look back. They stare at her eyes.

NARRATOR 1: "To stone!" Perseus cries. "Everyone! To stone!"

HEROES: Wow. Wow!

STUDENT: Done! Do you suppose they're petrified—in those stones—right in front of us? (*Pause*) Oh, maybe not. So, what happens to that head?

NARRATOR 1: Well, that's in another myth.

STUDENT: And Acrisius—is he still afraid of his own grandson?

NARRATOR 4: Look, go to the library! These stories continue on and on!

STUDENT: And the horse, Pegasus? Okay. I get it. Another myth. Well, this one will keep me company for a while—like in my nightmares! But I think I'll draw a picture of Medusa's head—those snakes were cool!

NARRATOR 1: And look up at the sky tonight. Perseus is a constellation, you know.

EXPLORER 2: Pegasus, too! Say, maybe we all need a book about Greek myths.

EXPLORER 1: More adventures ahead—myths around the world. Let's go!

HEROES: Wait! Wait! We're coming, too!

Myths from Around the World: India

Avatar Adventures with Vishnu

INTRODUCTION

Ancient stories, like ancient history, have an undeniable influence on our lives. For example, ancient oral myths permeate the written literature of India, to the extent that many have become part of the Hindu scriptures. Vishnu, one of three primary gods of ancient India, is still greatly honored for his mythical roles in preserving humankind.

We are always hampered in our search for ancient stories by the passage of time and by texts written in unfamiliar, often obsolete languages. Uncovering the stories of Vishnu means we must look back many thousands of years. And it would be helpful if we knew Vedic and Sanskrit, the written languages of the early Indian literature. Fortunately, others have already trod this path, and we can look to copious works from scholars on the philosophies and actions of the multifaceted god, Vishnu.

In his efforts to preserve mankind, Vishnu at times adopted the guise of an avatar, appearing on Earth at judicious moments in one of nine unexpected forms, such as a tortoise or a boar or a creature that was half man and half lion. In this way, he was able to quell chaos on Earth promptly, wisely, and with surprise. His actions, although sometimes violent, always contributed to the good of mankind. It is believed that Vishnu's tenth avatar, still to come, will establish a new era for mankind in the future.

The numerous stories of Vishnu lead us into a vast number of philosophical writings, lessons, poems, and epics, such as *The Mahabharata* and *The Ramayana,* the story of Rama, Vishnu's seventh avatar. Highly revered, these writings are considered sacred and have become an integral part of Hindu literary and religious life.

PRODUCTION NOTES

Character transformations in literature often allow new events to take place, cause relationships to change, and direct mystical power to other beings. The avatars of Vishnu are replete with such sudden and mysterious gifts. We don't fully understand these transformed beings, but we can appreciate their function in the myths from ancient India. Certainly, we can enjoy bringing them alive in spirited oral readings based on the classic Hindu scriptures.

The following script calls for fifteen students; however, to cast fewer Ashramas, lines can be combined. Essentially, sixteen scripts are necessary, including one for the teacher.

The five Ashramas (students of Hindu) serve as a Chorus of response. They comment on the actions and emotions portrayed in the script. Occasionally an individual Ashrama will pose a question to propel the plot along.

The Elder One and the god Vishnu provide explanations of the story and weave the narrative threads.

Avatars 1–6 present their roles in the hierarchy of the god Vishnu. Each is different; each has a dramatic anecdote to reveal. Thus, voices can vary with each student's imagination. For example, Avatar 2 is a tortoise and not likely to have the gruff voice of the boar, Avatar 3. Avatar 4 might show his cunning nature and pride in his voice and attitude. Avatars 5 and 6 have similar challenges and possibilities in their lines.

Avatar 7 (Rama) holds a special place in these adventures, for he emerged as a human, and hopefully he will sound more calm and mature than the others.

Dasharatha, the mortal father of Rama, is a responsible monarch in need of a son, and as such is both an anxious king and, eventually, a grateful one.

Avatar Adventures with Vishnu

Avatar Adventures with Vishnu

Mythical Tales from India

```
                          Ashramas A–E
                          X X X X X
Avatars1, 2, 3                              Avatars 4, 5, 6
X X X                                       X X X
         Avatar 7 (Rama)              Dasharatha
         X                            X

     Vishnu                      Elder One
     X                           X
```

ALL ASHRAMAS: *Soft, sustained sound of "OM" during the next four speeches*

VISHNU: Who are those people behind us, Old One, and what are they saying?

ELDER ONE: Oh, Vishnu, those are your followers—the young ashramas, such special students! They chant for you! (*ahsh-rah'-mahs*) (*Vish'nu*)

VISHNU: Yes, yes. But after ten thousand years, I seem to grow a bit weary. (*Sighs*) Burdens, you know—and so many adventures.

ELDER ONE: Perhaps it is the students, Vishnu. (*Calls gently*) Ashrama! Enough.

ALL ASHRAMAS: *On the "Enough," all become silent.*

ELDER ONE: Better, eh?

VISHNU: Much better—and now no more traveling!

ELDER ONE: Sorry, Lord Vishnu—you do have another adventure! This time, however, the ashramas join your presence with great eagerness.

ASHRAMA A: Elder One, tell us about Vishnu. Who is that? Exactly, *who*?

ELDER ONE: Infidel! You ask *who* is the god Vishnu? Surely you know Vishnu—the Great Preserver, the Lord of the Universe!

ASHRAMA B: No, but I think we get it: Vishnu is a major god. So, he must do something special—all gods do special things. What does Vishnu do?

VISHNU: It is difficult to explain. (*Pause*) Basically, my purpose is to preserve mankind. So I destroy demons, and I protect all people who are good.

ASHRAMA C: Obviously *what* he does is good, but *when* did these deeds take place? Do we have a Vishnu Period? A date? An era? A time? When?

ELDER ONE: Our myths start in the Beginning—when, they said, our entire universe was under water.

ASHRAMA D: I see we're set for an adventure, but *where* to?

VISHNU: We go to a magical place. Everyone, you must come! Come with me to a faraway, long ago, mystical India.

ASHRAMA E: India. Faraway, yes. Long ago, okay. But mystical? *Why*?

ELDER ONE: It's simple. Come, witness the creation of the world—with Vishnu.

ASHRAMA D: That sounds spectacular! How does the god Vishnu do that?

ELDER ONE: Good question, and the answer lies in our ancient myths. One Vishnu—many shapes.

ASHRAMA C: You're kidding. This Lord Vishnu has many shapes? How is this possible? Explain, please.

VISHNU: They're my avatars. You know, *avatars*? I have ten so far.

ASHRAMA B: I know avatars are *like* you, but they're *not* you—exactly. They're not copies, either. That's about all I know. But I definitely don't know *your* avatars. Do they look like you?

VISHNU: Certainly not!

AVATAR 1: Excuse me. (*Bows head briefly*) I am called Matsya, Lord Vishnu's first avatar—starting as a very small golden fish.(*Mat-see'-yah*)

ELDER ONE: Very small when the sea waves were small—before the winds began to blow—before black rain fell from the clouds—before the waters began to rise.

AVATAR 1: Demons filled the sea! Chaos was about to rule! I began to change. My body grew thicker, longer, stronger! My golden fins flashed like fire. My tail snapped and whipped through the waters like a deadly blade. I knew that a man was in danger!

VISHNU: Not just any man, of course, but one called Manu—Manu, who had been a king. My mission, as Matsya, was to warn him. The Deluge was coming!

ELDER ONE: A giant flood was coming to wipe out all mankind.

AVATAR 1: Evil was boiling in the waters. The pores in my body were exploding!

ASHRAMA E: But you're only a fish!

AVATAR 1: Not so. Not so! The power of Vishnu raced through my blood. I had a mission. I, alone, had to tell the king that he must build a huge boat, then gather two of every living creature, gather the seeds and roots of every flower and tree. All these must be on the ship with him.

ASHRAMA C: And the flood came to pass—and only that ship was saved?

VISHNU: The rains did cease, and the winds died down. Manu's ship rested on a tall, tall mountain. Manu had been spared. As a good man, he would start a new race of people to thrive and grow. Mankind was preserved.

ALL ASHRAMAS: *Soft, brief, sustained sound of "OM"*

ELDER ONE: Vishnu was able to preserve mankind this time, but the Deluge was not the end of things. Indeed, it came to pass that Vishnu again sensed trouble.

VISHNU: The gods in our kingdom were discontented. They wished to live forever. If they could drink just one drop of the magic potion, *amrita (ahm-ree'-tah)*, they would never die.

ASHRAMA D: Who had this magic potion? Couldn't they get it, somehow?

VISHNU: The potion lay within the Ocean of Milk. Only by churning that ocean would the *amrita* emerge.

AVATAR 2: The time was ripe for me—Kurma, second avatar for Lord Vishnu.

ASHRAMA E: Now *you* have a completely different shape—you're a tortoise. That's odd. We all know the tortoise is a very slow reptile.

VISHNU: Yes, but the tortoise is also blessed with a very hard shell.

ELDER ONE: A most useful covering in this adventure. It begins with a churn.

AVATAR 2: Of course, every churn has to have a paddle to stir with, so to stir up the Ocean of Milk, they set the great mountain Mandara upon my back, and that mountain became the paddle. Next, the great snake Vasuki became the rope. (*Vah-sue'-kee*)

ELDER ONE: And the churning and the swirling began. The ocean heaved and bubbled with froth. For a thousand years they churned.

AVATAR 2: Suddenly, out came the Sun, then the Moon, and the goddess of fortune, bearing stars and precious jewels.

VISHNU: At last the divine physician appeared, bearing the magic potion of immortality for the gods, the *amrita*.

ALL ASHRAMAS: *Soft, brief sustained sound of "OM"*

AVATAR 3: That's all very well for the gods, but as Vishnu, I, too, helped mankind. I, Varaha, the third avatar, came in the shape of a boar.

ASHRAMA A: A boar? Boars are clumsy beasts with a tough, bristly hide and long, curved tusks. What can they do for mankind?

AVATAR 3: You forgot to mention my extraordinary sense of smell, or that I could plunge to the depths of the ocean. I killed a demon resting down there with just my tusks. Then I brought back the earth imprisoned in the waves of the ocean.

ELDER ONE: Noble deeds, all in the interests, the service of mankind. Ashrama?

ALL ASHRAMAS: *Very brief "OM"*

AVATAR 4: Don't forget the demon I killed—that heinous king who wanted to kill his own son, Prahlada. It was I who killed that demon king, I, Narasinka, Lord Vishnu's fourth avatar. (*Prah-lah-dah*) (*Nar-a-sink-a*)

ELDER ONE: The king was truly a demon, but he had special immunity.

AVATAR 4: He did—threefold: He could not be killed by a man or a beast or a god. He could not be killed in the daytime or at night. And third, he could not be killed *inside* or outside his house.

98

ELDER ONE:	How could you overcome his immunity to death?
VISHNU:	By careful planning. This demon was killed by my avatar Narasinka, who came to the demon king not as a man or a beast or a god, but as a creature—half man, half lion.
AVATAR 4:	And I came not at night nor in the daytime, but at *evening*. Then I appeared at the *entrance* to the king's palace, neither inside nor out. When the evil king appeared, I, Narsinka, stepped forward and *ripped* the demon to pieces, preserving the son Prahlada and his line.
ALL ASHRAMAS:	*Brief chant of "OM"*
ASHRAMA B:	Avatars seem to be big and powerful and ruthless.
ELDER ONE:	You've left out *brilliant, compassionate,* and *clever.*
AVATAR 5:	Which, at long last, brings you to me, the fifth avatar, Vamana.
ELDER ONE:	And, to the reign of Prahlada's grandson, Bali. (*Bah-lee'*)
VISHNU:	Bali was not a bad king. He treated his people well, and he honored the gods—up to a point. Then his greedy ambition took over.
ELDER ONE:	Bali had claimed all the land on Earth that he could. Now he was looking to take even more land in the kingdom of the gods.
ASHRAMA A:	Conquering such a powerful king certainly calls for a huge avatar.
AVATAR 5:	Not necessarily. I appeared before King Bali as a *dwarf*, and counting on his generous nature, I asked for a gift of land, three paces long.
ASHRAMA A:	As a dwarf, you would take three steps, and that would measure the land you wanted? That doesn't sound like very much.

AVATAR 5: It wasn't much. The king approved the gift, until, that is, I proceeded to grow bigger and bigger and bigger. I was no longer a dwarf.

ASHRAMA A: I see! As you grew, your paces, or strides, grew bigger and bigger.

VISHNU: They did, and as they did, the size of the land increased a hundred times. Bali's greed collapsed. He'd learned his lesson the hard way.

ELDER ONE: As did the warriors of another tribe who killed and robbed at will.

AVATAR 6: As Parashurama, the sixth avatar of Lord Vishnu, I fought these cruel warriors in twenty-one campaigns. I killed all their men with my axe, a special axe—a gift of the gods. (*Pahr-a-sure-a-rah-ma*)

VISHNU: The blood of those slain warriors filled five large lakes. (*Brief sigh*) Despite these victories, mankind was still in danger. Now King Ravana, a demon with ten heads, was threatening both gods and men.

ASHRAMA B: So you sent another avatar, like the lion man or maybe the boar?

VISHNU: No. King Ravana could not be killed by any other *demons*, any of the *gods*, or any of the *spirits*. Only a *man* could kill him.

AVATAR 7: And the only god who could take the human form was Lord Vishnu. So he did, and his human form became me, Rama, the seventh avatar.

ASHRAMA C: Becoming a human must mean you were born of human parents.

VISHNU: Special parents who desired a child—someone like King Dasharatha. (*Dahsh-ah-rah-tha*)

ELDER ONE: King Dasharatha had his three wives, but they had been childless for many years. That meant the king had no one to inherit his throne.

DASHARATHA: I was desperate. I even consulted the wise men of my city for help. After many prayers, they ordered me to make special offerings.

VISHNU: Remember, Dasharatha was a true believer and a good man.

ASHRAMA D: Well, I'm guessing the special offerings worked.

DASHARATHA: They did! Not long after that, all three of my wives became pregnant. Soon I was blessed with four sons, Rama being the first born.

ASHRAMA D: And Rama, when you grew up, did you have several wives, too?

AVATAR 7: No, no. I won the beautiful Sita for my wife—my only wife.

ASHRAMA D: You *won* her? How? Was she a prize or something?

AVATAR 7: Actually, yes, in a competition. The god Shiva had given her father a miraculously strong bow, and it was he who set up the competition. He said that whoever could bend that bow could marry his daughter, Sita. I had seen her, and I was most desirous of winning that contest.

ELDER ONE: Too modest, Rama. You actually broke that miraculous bow.

DASHARATHA: He did. He did! The lovely Sita joined our family, and now I felt content. I was ready to abdicate the throne in favor of my son, Rama.

ELDER ONE: But all was not well. One of Dasharatha's wives spelled trouble. She wanted *her* son, Bharata, to become king, not Rama. (*Bah-rah-tah*)

VISHNU: The four sons of Dasharatha had no jealousy for each other's position. *They* worked and played together as one. It was one of the *mothers* who was too ambitious.

ELDER ONE: She tricked King Dasharatha. She asked him for a favor. But before he realized her treachery, he granted her the favor. And now the damage was done.

DASHARATHA: I was forced to make *her* son, Bharata, the new king instead of Rama. Worse. I had to send Rama into exile for fourteen years.

AVATAR 7: Our people were devastated, but I understood what had happened. Yet I could do nothing. Sita, my wife, went into exile with me—my brother, Lakshmana, too. (*Lahk-shmah-nah*)

ASHRAMA C: That must have been disastrous!

AVATAR 7: No, I knew we would survive, even in the forest. My father, though (*Pause*), my father died in a week—of a broken heart, they say.

ASHRAMA C: So Bharata became king?

AVATAR 7: Yes, but we were very close. I knew he had nothing to do with his mother's trickery. He begged me to return home, but I was honor-bound to stay in exile. So he ruled as regent, but he kept my rightful position alive.

ASHRAMA D: Fourteen years in exile! What happened to everybody in the forest?

VISHNU: Surpanakha is what happened. (*Sir-pahn-ahk'-ha*)

ELDER ONE: Evil happened. She was the very picture of evil—a huge, ugly giantess, a creature of darkness, an enemy of men, and the sister of that ten-headed demon king, Ravana.

VISHNU: Surpanakha found them in the forest, of course, but when she appeared before them, she had worked her own magic. She was no longer the huge, ugly giantess, covered with warts and greasy hair. She had made herself beautiful!

AVATAR 7: Surpanakha. She was a stranger with a strange name. We tried to be friendly and to make her comfortable in our simple ashram.

VISHNU: They were too agreeable, far too agreeable. They didn't know the giantess was a demon!

ASHRAMA D: Was she friendly, too?

ELDER ONE: So friendly that Surpanakha said she was in love with Rama. She wanted him to leave his wife, Sita, and come live with her.

AVATAR 7: Even though she'd changed from her ugliness, I choked at the thought of being with her! But then I had an idea. She *was* beautiful then. Maybe my brother, Lakshmana, would like her for a wife.

ASHRAMA D: Now there's a thought.

AVATAR 7: But my brother said no and laughed at the idea. That made Surpanakha furious! She thought that he, too, was in love with Sita, and that's why he'd turned her down. Well, she gave my Sita such a look of hatred, I thought Surpanakha might kill her.

ASHRAMA C: What did you do?

AVATAR 7: I pulled Sita close to me. Then the demon swore she'd kill Sita—and eat her!

VISHNU: At those words, Lakshmana seized his knife. Balancing the carved bone handle in his powerful grip, he ran his fingers down the blade, feeling its smoothness, checking its keenness. Then, in one swift movement, Lakshmana cut off the nose and both ears of the crazed giantess, the evil demon, Surpanakha.

ALL ASHRAMA: *Whew!*

ASHRAMA A: End of story?

ELDER ONE: Hardly, my friends. A myth is only the beginning. The stories grow, become ever more interesting, ever more humorous. They tell us more about us—what we believe, and how we should act.

ASHRAMA B: I can't believe these stories get written down.

ASHRAMA E: Infidel! They become epics!

ELDER ONE: Good thinking! The story of Sita, Rama, and his brothers grew into a famous epic called *Ramayana*—the *Epic of Rama*, Prince of India.

VISHNU: The poets tell the story. Book One in the Veda begins like this: "Rich in royal worth and valour, rich in holy Vedic lore, Dasaratha ruled his empire in the happy days of yore . . ."

ELDER ONE: Full circle, Lord Vishnu. It's time. Ashramas?

ALL ASHRAMAS: *Soft, sustained sound of "OM" until Vishnu leaves the stage*

Myths from Around the World: Ireland

An Ancient Irish Hero, Cuchulain

INTRODUCTION

Oh, the names, the names! We dredge up the ancient Celtic past, and we come up with the likes of Ibar, Conchubar, Conall, and Culain—and then Cuchulain, our Irish hero. These strange names certainly do not roll "trippingly on the tongue," as Hamlet might have wished, but probing into their stories is surely part of the adventure of reading. In this case, we are reading aloud ancient tales that William Butler Yeats called "a chief part of Ireland's gift to the imagination of the world."

The first Celtic people are thought to have appeared in Ireland during the Iron Age (about 600 BC), migrating from Greece, Europe, and Britain. With the advent of Christianity in the fifth century, a literary heritage began to evolve, one that scholars today recognize as being unique for its clarity, details, and richness.

As all myths seem to be a compendium of life experiences and early beliefs, it's natural that they should become more and more fulsome with time and their eventual recording. Imagine Cuchulain, perhaps near his ceremonial home on the Hill of Tara, when he takes up arms and proclaims, "I swear by the oath of my people, I will make my doings be spoken of among the great doings of heroes in their strength."

Echoes of such firm Irish resolve continue to appear even in today's literature. Think of Scarlett O'Hara as she stands near her plantation home, Tara, and proclaims, "As God is my witness, I will never be hungry again!"

Kings, druids, warriors, and a god who becomes a mayfly enlarge the heroic myth of Cuchulain. The fanciful folklore of leprechauns, banshees, and fairies will come later!

PRODUCTION NOTES

Legends grow from the many myths that have sprung up about the renowned prowess of the warrior hero from ancient Ulster, Cuchulain. Surrounded by druids, order, fantasy, intelligence, obedience, and magic, this miraculous child, then man, is literally larger than life. Yet he is human, and therefore he is especially honored and revered.

The following script about Cuchulain calls for a cast of twelve readers and two crew members to handle the sound effects. A total of fifteen scripts will be needed, which includes one for the teacher.

Explorers 1 and 2 act as our guides. In general, Explorer 1 is more on top of things, whereas Explorer 2 is a little slow, more questioning.

Druids 1–5 have become narrators for this adventure. They supply information, interpret other speeches, and often stimulate the action.

Conchubar, from Ulster, is one of the feudal kings of ancient Ireland. Basically strong, he is almost always in control, and oversees most of the action.

Culain, a blacksmith, can be pretty emotional. He is subservient to Conchubar but becomes very upset over the loss of his hound.

Ibar is steady and confident, but mindful of his responsibility for Cuchulain.

Conall, older than Cuchulain, is protective of his younger, impetuous cousin.

Cuchulain, our Irish hero, is confident, brave, and competent. His words and actions may seem over the top, but he does what he promises—no question about that!

Sound effects are explained in the script; however, they can be eliminated without harming the effect of the story.

An Ancient Irish Hero, Cuchulain

An Ancient Irish Hero, Cuchulain

Celtic Mythical Tales

```
                          Sounds A, B
                             X, X
      Ibar            Culain              Explorer1   Explorer2
       X                X                    X           X
      Conall      Conchubar              Cuchulain              Druids 1–5
       X            X                       X                    X X X X X
```

SOUND A: (*Loud metallic noises—pans rattle; hammers strike iron pot.*)

EXPLORER 1:   Man! What is going on?

EXPLORER 2:   Just checking my weaponry.

EXPLORER 1:   We're in the middle of Dublin, Ireland, and you're checking your weaponry? Because—hey, you *do* have a cause?

EXPLORER 2:   It's that stone pillar we saw, the one standing in the post office.

EXPLORER 1:   Ah, yes—Cuchulain's pillar. Now, *there's* a story to tell. (*Ku-ku-lin'*)

EXPLORER 2:   Okay, so tell already! All I know is he was some kind of a hero.

EXPLORER 1:   He was a warrior—a real hero! Check out those Druids. They could tell you. Remember? They were like priests, teachers, poets, judges . . . .

EXPLORER 2: Cool. Call a couple of them up. Let's hear what they have to say.

SOUND B: (*Reed flute plays a few notes, then gradually fades under Druid 1.*)

DRUID 1: We're here, lads, and sure it's a strange country you're livin' in today. Not like the grand old days, back, *way* back, maybe two or three thousands years, back when the lad Cuchulain became our hero.

DRUID 2: *Then* you could see weaponry—Cuchulain's *real* weaponry, like his javelin, his *gae bolga*, for instance. (*gaay boll'-jah*)

DRUID 3: Sure, and that spelled death for the enemy, for when the *gae bolga* struck a man, it wasn't the point that wounded him; it was the thirty sharp barbs that burst from the spear, twisting and ripping his insides.

DRUID 1: It was fierce, gory! But don't be forgetting his shield, the Black One.

DRUID 3: Or his sword. That sword was so brilliant that it glowed in the dark and so sharp it could cut a hair on water—or cut a man in two.

DRUID 4: The half left would not even miss his other half until hours later.

EXPLORER 2: That's pretty unbelievable.

EXPLORER 1: So where does this pillar come in? What does it mean?

DRUID 1: Mean? Ah, strength. Courage! Defiance! Sacrifice! Patriotism!

DRUID 2: I expect they want to hear about Cuchulain, from the beginning.

DRUID 3: And what a story! A boy who's a hero when he's but seven years old!

DRUID 4: It started with the Ulster king Conchubar and his sister. (*Kon-ku-bar*)

CONCHUBAR: She swallowed a mayfly in her drink, and soon after had a baby boy. She named him Setanta, after her husband. (*Seh-tant'-a*)

DRUID 4: (*Whispers*) His name, Cuchulain, came later. Even so, some said his father was really the god Lugh. (*Loog*)

DRUID 3: (*Whispers*) True! We all heard he'd appeared to her as that mayfly.

DRUID 5: Well, certainly from the beginning, Setanta was a miracle child.

CONCHUBAR: I wanted my other sister to bring him up. Alas, many fought for that privilege—my druids and chiefs alike.

DRUID 1: Even our chief judge and poet wanted that honor. He said, "It is not for that woman to bring up this child. No, it is for *me*!"

DRUID 4: (*Whispers*) We had to listen to him!

DRUID 5: We listened, even when he bragged, saying, "I am skilled. I am good in disputes. I am not forgetful. I speak before anyone at all in the presence of the king. I watch over what he says, and I give judgment in the quarrels of kings. I am the judge for the men of Ulster. No one has a right to dispute *my* claim—only King Conchubar himself."

DRUID 2: Whew! Then one of the chieftains stepped in, he with his big voice: "I always follow the king's wishes. I called up the men of Ireland. I settled their disputes. I supported their honor. This child will never suffer from want of care or forgetfulness from me!"

DRUID 4: But then the king's messenger shoved the chieftain aside and spoke *his* own piece: "You think too much of yourself," he said. "It is I that will bring up the child. I am strong. I have knowledge."

DRUID 5: Well, of course, he was important. He was the king's messenger. It was hard to get the better of him in honor *or* in riches.

DRUID 4: And he kept pressing his case, saying, "I am hardened to war and battles. I am a good craftsman. I am the protector of all the unhappy. The strong are afraid of me. I am the helper of the weak. *I* am worthy to bring up a child!"

DRUID 3: Silence fell. Then it was the tutor's turn. He said, " So, you will listen to me at last, now that you are quiet."

EXPLORER 1: That's a sharp tongue the tutor has!

DRUID 5: A sharp tongue, but little modesty. Then, not caring whether they listened or not, he said, "*I* am able to bring up a child like a king."

DRUID 3: And he went on: "The people praise my honor, my bravery, my courage, my wisdom, my good luck, my age, my speaking, my name, and my family. Though I am a fighter, I am a poet."

DRUID 5: True enough, but he had still more to say: "I am worthy of the king's favor. I overcome all men who fight from their chariots. I owe thanks to no one except Conchubar. I obey no one except the king."

EXPLORER 2: Not easy to make a decision, huh? They're all perfect!

DRUID 1: Well, the final judge decreed that the baby should live with the king's sister, the baby's aunt—still, all would share in his upbringing.

CONCHUBAR: And he added, "This child, Setanta, will be praised and loved by all—by chariot drivers and fighters, kings and wise men. He will avenge your wrongs. He will defend your forts and fight all your battles."

CUCHULAIN: So I was sent to live with my aunt and her son Conall, near the King's court—so close to it, I could hear the boys playing games. (*Con'-ull*)

CONCHUBAR: Setanta wanted to join in their games, but my sister said he was too young. That didn't stop him, though he was only seven.

CUCHULAIN: They were playing a game with a ball. I stepped onto their field, and when the ball came near to me, I drove it along with my feet and sent it flying, past the goal. Great cries of anger poured from those boys.

EXPLORER 1: Oh, that was a major error—interfering with somebody else's game.

EXPLORER 2: He's in deep trouble!

CUCHULAIN: At first I was. They came after me with everything they had, but I rushed *them*, and I threw them all to the ground.

EXPLORER 1: He did that when he was seven? You're right—he was a miracle.

CONCHUBAR: I chastised the boy for fighting on the playground. But this powerful lad was my sister's son, so I brought him into my house to live.

CULAIN: The king was proud of Setanta—of his strength and courage. He even wanted to bring him to a feast at my house. But the boy hung back.

CUCHULAIN: Please, don't wait for me. I can follow the tracks of your chariot later to the blacksmith's house. I know the smithy Culain well. (*Coo-linn'*)

CULAIN: So the king came on alone. He joined in the feasting and drinking and dancing, but I asked him, "Was anyone coming late to the party?"

CONCHUBAR: No, Culain. Why do you ask me that?

CULAIN: Because I have a great fierce hound dog, and when I remove his chain, he lets no one come onto my grounds. He will obey no one but myself. I warn you, he has the strength of a hundred hounds.

CONCHUBAR: Oh, release him, Culain. Let him keep his usual watch on your place.

DRUID 1: Hard to believe, but the king had forgotten Setanta was coming later.

SOUND A: (*Low, ominous growling*)

CUCHULAIN: Finally, I struck out for Culain's house, carrying my stick and ball. But as I approached, the hound dog, asleep on the lawn, heard me.

SOUND A: (*Growling grows louder, more intense.*)

CUCHULAIN: Then he sprang at me—his great, wet, slobbery mouth raged at me like a black dragon. I had no weapon at all, but I knew those jaws wanted to tear me apart, to swallow me like a chunk of raw meat.

EXPLORER 2: What did he do? Good grief, he's only seven years old!

EXPLORER 1: With nothing but his playing stick and a ball—no weapons!

DRUID 1: Well, the lad drove that ball toward the hound with such force that the ball went right down the hound's throat and clear through his body.

DRUID 2: Then he seized the hound by the hind legs and dashed him against a rock until there was no life left in him.

SOUND A: (*Growling stops.*)

CONCHUBAR: We heard the outcry of the hound, and *then* I remembered Setanta! We rushed outside, dreading to see what had happened to my nephew.

CULAIN: Setanta was fine, but when I saw my great hound dead, I was filled with grief. I said, "That was a good member of my family you took from me. He was the protector of my goods and my flocks and my herds—indeed, of all that I have." But Setanta's answer startled us.

CUCHULAIN: Do not be vexed. I myself will make up to you for what I have done.

CONCHUBAR: That's impossible, I thought, and I said so. But the boy was firm.

CUCHULAIN: This is how I will do it. If there is a young dog of the same breed to be had in Ireland, I will rear him and train him until he is as good a hound as the one you see lying there.

CULAIN: I was dumbfounded, listening to him.

CUCHULAIN: And *until* the time I deem him ready, I, myself, will be your hound, your watchdog. I will guard your goods, your cattle, and your house.

CONCHUBAR: Culain was appeased at this, and from this time on Setanta was known by his new name. *Now* he was called Cuchulain, the Hound of Culain.

DRUID 3: And we druids prophesied that all men would someday have the name of Cuchulain in their mouths.

EXPLORER 1: But what did the little Hound do next?

DRUID 3: Nothing, until one day the tutor told his pupils, "If any young man should take arms today, his name will be greater than any other in Ireland. But," he cautioned, "if he does, his life will be short."

SOUND A: (*Metallic noises briefly—pans rattle; hammer strikes iron pot.*)

EXPLORER 2: Take arms? Does that mean to get his weapons, or to fight?

DRUID 2: Both! Once you have your weapons, you must prove yourself. You must use your arms, and use them with valor!

EXPLORER 2: Talk about destiny. Not much chance for the would-be warrior!

CUCHULAIN: I heard my tutor's prediction, and I went straight to King Conchubar.

CONCHUBAR: And what is it that you are wanting today?

114

CUCHULAIN: I want to take arms. Our tutor has said that whoever takes arms today, his name will be greater than any other in Ireland. He didn't speak of the harm to come. He said only that the warrior's life would be short.

CONCHUBAR: Think again, Cuchulain. If you take arms, there will be fame for you and a great name, but your lifetime will not be long.

CUCHULAIN: It is little I would care if my life were to last only one day and one night, so long as my name and my story would live after me.

EXPLORER 1: Brave words—but a dangerous omen, I would think.

DRUID 1: But splendid arms, for only the arms and the chariot and horses of King Conchubar were fine enough, strong enough, for Cuchulain.

DRUID 2: Even Ibar, the king's charioteer, was sent to guide him. (*Ee-bar*)

IBAR: We set out with the horses, even as I urged caution on the young boy.

CUCHULAIN: No, Ibar! No fear! Let us drive on to where the boys are at play, so they may wish me good luck on the day of my taking arms.

IBAR: So we did, and they cheered and shouted, "Do well in the wounding. Be first in the killing and in winning spoils." After all that, I wanted to turn the horses loose to graze, but Cuchulain wouldn't hear of it.

CUCHULAIN: Too soon, good Ibar! Look ahead, and tell me where that road leads.

IBAR: To the watchers' ford. Each day a champion warrior keeps watch there in case any stranger may come to challenge the boundary line.

CUCHULAIN: Ah! Do you know which warrior is on watch today?

IBAR: I know well it is Conall, the chief champion of the young men of Ulster and of all Ireland.

CUCHULAIN: My foster brother! Excellent! Let us not loiter. On to the ford!

IBAR: So we struck out, and at the water's edge, we found Conall.

CONALL: Well, well. And are those arms you have taken today, little boy?

IBAR: I will answer for him, Conall. They are arms, indeed.

CONALL: May they bring him triumph and victory and shedding of the first blood. But I think, little Hound, you are too eager to take arms. You are not fit as yet to do a champion's work.

CUCHULAIN: What is it you are doing here, Conall?

CONALL: I'm keeping watch. I guard the boundary line for our province.

CUCHULAIN: Step aside, Conall, and for this one day, let me keep watch.

CONALL: Oh, no, little one. You cannot stand against trained fighting men.

CUCHULAIN: Then I will go to our enemies at Echtra to redden my arms. (*Ek-tra*)

CONALL: Ah, I see. Then I will go with you—to protect you, for if I let you go into a strange country alone, all of Ulster would avenge this on me.

IBAR: Conall yoked his horses to his chariot and made ready to leave. But Cuchulain would not wait for him. We started out for Echtra at once.

CUCHULAIN: Suddenly, I saw Conall close behind us. I thought that if I did get a chance to do something great, Conall would never let me do it.

IBAR: Before I knew it, Cuchulain had picked up a stone the size of his fist and hurled it at the yoke of Conall's chariot. The yoke broke, the chariot came down, and Conall was thrown sideways to the ground.

CONALL: (*Furiously*) What did you do that for?

CUCHULAIN: To see if there was the making of a good champion in me.

CONALL: Well, bad luck on your throwing and on yourself! And anyone who likes may strike your head off now! I will go with you no further!

CUCHULAIN: That is just what I wanted!

DRUID 4: Ah, that was the beginning. Soon the arms of little Hound reddened with the blood of three brothers, all ruthless killers of Ulstermen.

DRUID 3: Carrying the bleeding heads home in his chariot, Cuchulain stopped to outrun a herd of deer, caught two stags, and bound them to the chariot. Then he captured sixteen wild swans and tied them there, too.

DRUID 1: And in every battle he fought, there was never anyone like him!

DRUID 2: Whenever he fought, he became consumed with a battle frenzy. His body would shake all over. He seemed to revolve within his skin.

DRUID 3: His face would turn red. One eye would grow huge, the other, tiny!

DRUID 4: His mouth would open wide. Then a shower of sparks would fly out. His hair spiked, and a glowing warrior light shone from his brow.

EXPLORER 1: He sounds invincible! Who could even touch him in battle?

DRUID 1: (*Slowly*) No one. Not then—or since. No one—of *this* world.

EXPLORER 2: What does that mean? Another world? Interference from the gods?

DRUID 1: Magic—tricks by a queen that Cuchulain had conquered many times.

DRUID 2: King Conchubar heard of the evil queen's plans. He tried to protect Cuchulain, but he failed. (*Pause*) Three deadly javelins struck home.

DRUID 4: The first killed Cuchulain's charioteer. The second, Grey, his mighty horse. The third went through and through Cuchulain's body.

DRUID 5: They say his bowels spilled out on the cushions of the chariot, and his only remaining horse, Black Sainglain (*Sin-glin*), went away from him, with half the harness hanging from his neck. He left his master, the king of the heroes of Ireland, to die.

SOUND B: (*Reed flute plays briefly and throughout the following speech.*)

DRUID 3: Cuchulain's eye lit upon a great pillar stone standing to the west of him. He went to the pillar, and with his belt, tied himself to it. He would not meet his death lying down; he would meet it standing up.

DRUID 1: Now his enemies came round about him, but they were in dread of going close to him, for they were not sure but that he might still be alive.

CONCHUBAR: Then, they say, a bird came, a raven, and it settled on his shoulder, and now they knew. And the enemy chieftain came up. He lifted Cuchulain's hair from his shoulders—and he struck off his head.

DRUID 1: Cuchulain's foster brother was filled with rage. It was now he, Conall, who would seek satisfaction for the death of Cuchulain, the Irish hero, whose deeds are still spoken of among the great deeds of great heroes.

Myths from Around the World: Scandinavia

The Taste of Dragon's Blood

INTRODUCTION

What makes an extraordinary man? In *Twelfth Night,* Shakespeare goads Malvolio with one memorable description: "Some are born great, some achieve greatness, and some have greatness thrust upon them." A fair-enough definition for most. Siegfried, however, is unique, for he represents a combination of these qualities. He had a remarkable birth, performed incredible exploits, and satisfied his inevitable destiny.

Legendary references to his birth are sprinkled with qualifications such as "it is said that" and "tradition suggests," because in truth, his story has emerged from a blending of oral traditions and early recorded history. From mythical beginnings, his birth and his exploits took root in the early Norse sagas (twelfth century), where he was known as Sigurd the Dragon Slayer and was considered an ancestor of the royal house of Norway.

As Sigurd's story became assimilated into early Germanic culture, the name and character of Sigurd changed to Siegfried, a hero thought to resemble an ancient Germanic god, powerful and invincible. Today we are most familiar with the blended tales of Sigurd/Siegfried in Richard Wagner's four-opera cycle, *The Ring of the Nibelungs.*

The German word *Nibelung* can refer to an early German dynasty or to the mythical race of gnomes who guarded a treasure of gold—treasure that became the Rhinegold of fables.

Because our hero is conceived as being great, he quite naturally achieves the greatness that is thrust upon him time and time again. This is his destiny. Yet he is vulnerable, and his tragic, inevitable death brings a sense of humanity to the stories of his godlike adventures.

PRODUCTION NOTES

The story of Siegfried, full of magic and power and impending disaster, cannot help but fascinate the imagination. With a strong dramatic oral reading of this myth, all these facets can come alive, and we begin to believe in an ancient time and mythical creatures.

Characters in the following script run the gamut from the volatile gnomes to the poets and King Charlemagne. Fourteen scripts will be needed, including those for the sound effects crew and the teacher.

Poets 1, 2, and 3 act as narrators. They suggest the literary recording of oral stories done by such early scribes.

The busy and officious Minstrels 1 and 2 narrate the main action of the story.

King Charlemagne presents a royal setting for us and an urgency for the telling of Siegfried's tale.

The Dragon speaks out loud and clear about his mission!

Siegfried, our hero, is, at turns, frightened, courageous, concerned, demanding, and above all, heroic.

Nibelungs 1, 2, and 3 represent the weird, mythical creatures who live and work in a mysterious underground world. They have skills and powers to be reckoned with. We hear that in their voices.

Sound effects are described in the script. They can be fun and are simple to execute, but they can be eliminated without any serious consequences.

The Taste of Dragon's Blood

The Taste of Dragon's Blood

Siegfried and the Nibelungs

	Sound A		Dragon		Sound B
	X		X		X
Poets 1, 2, 3	Minstrel 1	King Charlemagne		Minstrel 2	Nibelungs 1, 2, 3
X X X	X	X		X	X X X
		Siegfried			
		X			

SOUND A: (*Rhythmic drumbeats, firm, then softer during next three speeches*)

SOUND B: (*Rhythmic tinkle of bells accompanies the drumbeats.*)

MINSTREL 1: We have arrived, Your Majesty.

MINSTREL 2: At your service, King Charlemagne—at your beck and call and for all your wishes. (S*har-le-main*)

KING: (*Laughs*) Two minstrels? You? *You* will grant our wishes? (*Laughs*) Excellent! And, pray tell, how shall you accomplish all that for us? Have you a secret skill? Speak at once, bards!

SOUNDS A, B: (*Drums and bells stop abruptly.*)

MINSTREL 1: Your Majesty, with all due respect, we *have* brought you a secret.

From *More Readers Theatre for Middle School Boys: Adventures with Mythical Creatures* by Ann N. Black. Santa Barbara, CA: Teacher Ideas Press/Libraries Unlimited. Copyright © 2009.

MINSTREL 2: Of gold, sire—a secret of gold and power—and death.

KING: (*Laughs*) That's a heady mixture for such as you to tell.

SOUND A: (*Drumming begins again, slowly and ominously.*)

MINSTREL 1: The secret, sire, is not well known. It lies in the past and dwells with Siegfried and the Nibelungs. (*Seeg'-freed*) (*Nee'-ba-lungs*)

KING: The Nibelungs? From Burgundy? Aha! You have caught my interest—of stately matters elsewhere long before our reign.

MINSTREL 2: Of the state, perhaps, but deeper, Your Majesty—of the gnomes.

SOUND A: (*Drumming stops.*)

KING: More mysterious! Pray, have you the scrolls? Read them to us—now.

POET 3: Alas. There are no scrolls. Nothing is written down.

POET 2: The tale is but a myth. No one has recorded such a myth.

POET 1: Until now . . . we, the Poets, will try. Perhaps later men will read our feeble efforts. Then perhaps other poets will truly write this story.

KING: Excellent . . . but we cannot wait for such a manuscript. Time flees. Come, puppets, speak your piece. Fear not—tell the tale!

MINSTREL 2: Your Majesty, we bow to you, as we begin our tale of magic in this eighth century of our Lord, during your majesty's illustrious reign.

SOUND B: (*Bells begin to tinkle.*)

MINSTREL 1: "To us, in olden story, are wonders many told . . .

MINSTREL 2: Of heroes rich in glory—of trials manifold . . .

MINSTREL 1: Of joy and festive greeting—of weeping and of woe . . .

MINSTREL 2: Of keenest warriors meeting—shall you *now* many a wonder know."

SOUNDS A, B: (*Drumming with bells briefly, then both fade out as speeches begin.*)

POET 1: Start with Siegfried! Everybody loves a hero! (*Seeg'-freed*)

POET 2: Though we know not from whence this hero came.

POET 3: From the North country—that's enough, but of noble birth, indeed.

SIEGFRIED: 'Tis enough! I speak to you of mortal pain and the beautiful, the noble Kriemhild! Long did I yearn to meet her . . . to pursue her . . . to offer her my allegiance and my love! (*Kreem-hild*)

MINSTREL 1: But Kriemhild is a princess who lives far away—beyond the depths of the Black Forest, high in a dazzling city that teems with wealth and privilege . . . the city of Worms, on the banks of the shining Rhine River. (*Verms*)

MINSTREL 2: Ah, the Rhine—that sparkling stream of water rushing to the sea.

SIEGFRIED: I will find my way to Worms! I must find Kriemhild!

MINSTREL 1: Your lady, young Siegfried, is well protected by huge German warriors, and she is guarded especially by her brothers—Gunther, Gernot, and Giselher. (*Goon'-ter*) (*Ger'-not*) (*Ge'-sil-her*)

SIEGFRIED: Gunter, Gernot, and Giselher—the sons of King Gybich? Ah, I will remember those names. I will seek them out, and I will win them over with my words—or dispatch them with my sword! (*Guy-beek*)

KING: A brave man! This Siegfried—he is either brave or foolhardy. Which?

124

POET 1: We will take note—record the movements of this hero, Siegfried.

MINSTREL 2: We sing of Siegfried's life, Poet. Listen to the voice of our hero now.

SIEGFRIED: The day dawns bright and clear, but strong winds beckon to me. I must begin my journey—and somehow mend my father's magic sword, broken in his fierce battle of death. On this day I shall strike out for the distant East—and Kriemhild!

MINSTREL 1: And so he did. Gathering his cloak about him, Siegfried mounted his stalwart white steed and rode into the mists of an unknown land.

MINSTREL 2: The mists did swirl about him, gray and damp and foreboding. Night closed in. Thunder shook the land, but Siegfried was unafraid.

MINSTREL 1: Unafraid—until a strange rain came down—hard, white pellets, cold and wet. They struck his head like stones—scraped his face 'til it bled. He caught the pellets in his hand and tasted them. They dug furrows in his tongue like splinters of glass.

MINSTREL 2: What *was* this land? Where was he?

SOUND A: (*Muffled pounding of metal against metal, such as a blacksmith makes*)

SIEGFRIED: That sound on the wind—and that light I see! A friend? I care not! Friend or foe, I must find shelter, for my horse stumbles with pain.

MINSTREL 1: Siegfried bent low on his trusty steed and whispered in its ear. The horse reared, shook its head, but, bravely, it struggled on.

SOUND A: (*Pounding stops with a clash of metal.*)

NIBELUNG 1: (*Cackle of laughter*)

MINSTREL 1: Despite his courageous heart, Siegfried sensed *danger* ahead! He took a slow, deep breath, slid from his horse, and walked toward the dim glow—a ring of golden halos hovering above a great pile of stones.

MINSTREL 2: He moved closer to the sight, staggering with wonder and disbelief.

MINSTREL 1: Three small, ugly creatures crouched before him, barring the entrance to a cave. They wore short, ragged tunics and leather aprons.

MINSTREL 2: Their tools shone in the dark, hammers and picks for digging and tongs for working on an anvil. Miners they seemed and blacksmiths, but from another world. Then the ugliest of the gnomes stepped forward.

MINSTREL 1: Wild, shaggy hair covered his head and crept down his face like a fungus. Gobs of spittle dripped from his beard, which bristled with fury.

NIBELUNG 1: (*Cackle of laughter again*) So! You've arrived on our mountain, Siegfried. We are the Nibelungs. What do you seek from us? Coal from our mountain, I suppose? (*Cackles*) Fresh out!

NIBELUNG 2: (*Scornful laughter*) A noble man seeks help. What say you to that?

NIBELUNG 3: I say, "Throw him to the wolves! They howl. They're hungry!"

MINSTREL 1: Siegfried had to think fast. "These grotesque beings must be miners, maybe blacksmiths," he said to himself. "Maybe they *can* help me."

SIEGFRIED: Excuse me. May I rest my horse nearby? You see, I have with me a special sword—in two pieces. I understand that you work with iron and bronze. Perhaps . . . perhaps you can make my sword whole again?

MINSTREL 2: Siegfried loosened the pack on his horse and brought forth two large fragments of the magic sword he'd inherited from his warrior father.

NIBELUNG 2: That is a sword? (*Scornful laughter*) It's broken! It's in pieces!

SIEGFRIED: Yes, I know. But this is a very special sword. Can you restore it?

NIBELUNG 1: You are speaking to the Nibelungs. We are the artisans of this mountain. We labor for the gods, but all right, give the sword to me!

SOUND A: (*Drumbeats rise and fall three times, then a crash of metal*)

MINSTREL 1: The task was accomplished in an instant. The gnome left the forge, and carrying the now bright metal before him, brought the sword to Siegfried. The metal shone hot, as if fire still dwelt within the blade.

MINSTREL 2: Siegfried took the sword. He tested the hilt. He swung the weapon through the air. The blade trembled and sang three thin, high-pitched notes. With a curt nod, Siegfried pronounced the sword fit.

SIEGFRIED: Indeed, a yeoman's job. Well done!

KING: Forsooth, an artisan to admire! Is there more to your tale?

MINSTREL 1: Indeed, sire, for the sword held great magic for Siegfried now. He thrust it into its jeweled scabbard and prepared to mount his horse.

NIBELUNG 1: But what ceremony else? No thanks? No payment, sire?

SIEGFRIED: I pay you? Surely you jest! I will be on my way *now*.

NIBELUNG 2: (*Snorts in disgust*) He has no gold, brother. See—he is empty-handed. (*Slyly*) Perhaps . . . perhaps we can use him now.

MINSTREL 2: The strange little man hopped up and down. His skinny, twisted legs shot every which-way. His white eyeballs bulged with evil. They turned red, then black, then, streaked with blood, white again.

MINSTREL 1: The bearded one scratched his long, hooked nose, then his mangy head. What was he thinking? Siegfried waited. At last the Nibelung raised his scrawny arm.

NIBELUNG 1: (*Wheedling*) We want to help you, to talk about your service to us, and to talk about our gold.

SIEGFRIED: You are confused, Nibelung. It is *you* who must serve *me*, not I *you*!

NIBELUNG 2: (*Laughs slyly*) Until now—until now, Siegfried. Until now!

MINSTREL 1: The three spindle-legged dwarves barked and cackled like hyenas.

SIEGFRIED: I tarry no longer here. I must leave. Out of my way, Nibelungs!

NIBELUNG 1: Ah, so, Siegfried, leave! But first—look beyond, to the golden light.

POET 2: Now we come to the chapter on Treasures!

POET 3: You're thinking ahead again.

POET 1: It's appropriate. It's the history—the mystery—of the Rhinegold.

MINSTREL 1: Siegfried did look to the golden light again, and he began to feel a strange sensation—the light was drawing him closer, up the mountain.

NIBELUNG 2: (*Cackles*) He feels it, brother. The gold is sucking him in.

SIEGFRIED: What do you mean, gold?

NIBELUNG 3: There's gold for the asking up there . . . for the taking . . . for the killing.

SIEGFRIED: I don't understand. Whose gold is up there?

NIBELUNG 1: It's ours! Ours! The gold belongs to *us*, the Nibelungs.

NIBELUNG 2: (*Furious and excited*) It does! It does! He's the one who stole it! Him!

NIBELUNG 3: (*Furious*) And we can't get it back!

NIBELUNG 1: Quiet! (*Pause*) We will share the gold with you, on one condition.

MINSTREL 2: Siegfried was stunned. A real treasure would surely win him the beautiful Kriemhild. Yet how could he gain possession of this gold?

NIBELUNG 1: One condition, sire. Are you ready for this? A dragon guards the treasure—one who calls the treasure his. You must kill that dragon.

SOUND A: (*Muffled pounding of metal underlies next three lines.*)

SIEGFRIED: Kill a dragon? Impossible! They're not of this world. How *could* I?

NIBELUNG 2: You have your sword now.

NIBELUNG 3: You can kill it! Chop off its head!

MINSTREL 2: The challenge tore at Siegfried—until the pounding stopped, and the bearded one returned from his anvil with a newly fashioned helmet.

NIBELUNG 1: Take this helmet, warrior. Wear it. It will render you invisible.

NIBELUNG 2: And don't forget the ditch! You must dig a ditch—take this shovel.

SIEGFRIED: I have my sword, but I will take your shovel . . . and dig a ditch? Why?

NIBELUNG 3: (*Laughs with glee*) For the blood, Siegfried, the blood! Dig the ditch, then another. Dig two, or you will drown in the blood of the dragon.

MINSTREL 1: Crafty! They had thought of everything. Siegfried seized the shovel, donned the magic helmet, and set out for the dragon and the gold.

MINSTREL 2: A twisting, narrow path led up the mountainside. Little birds flew above him, ahead of him, singing wildly, leading him onward, as Siegfried began to climb into the glare of golden light.

SOUND A: (*Thrashing of branches*)

MINSTREL 1: Something was moving! He saw an enormous shadow rise before the light. The dragon! He'd found it! Hastily, Siegfried began to dig.

SOUND B: (*Stomping and wheezing*)

MINSTREL 2: Dirt and rocks and weeds flew through the air. Siegfried dug one long, winding ditch—then another, deeper than the first.

DRAGON: Stop, Siegfried! Step no closer, or my fire will sear your flesh and tear out your heart. I'll roast your liver 'til it's charred black as night.

SIEGFRIED: I care not for your threats, thief! I have come for the gold you guard.

DRAGON: The gold? It is my gold! It's in my den. The gold is mine!

SIEGFRIED: No! The Nibelungs cry foul! They say the gold is theirs—that you stole it. Now, soon, it will be my gold—*mine*.

DRAGON: Never! I will keep the magic—and the gold ring, for whoever wears that ring, rules the world. You'll never seize my gold—nor my ring!

MINSTREL 1: The huge, barbed serpent's tail rose through the branches searching for Siegfried. Flames shot from nostrils white hot. Smoke and cinders spewed from a mouth that oozed a thick, green, undulating foam.

SIEGFRIED: Come on, Dragon, show yourself. You frighten me not!

MINSTREL 2: The earth moaned and heaved. The huge beast was moving, sliding and thrashing. A thick, black fog shut out the world.

POET 1: Excuse me, but Siegfried was invisible, wasn't he?

POET 2: Of course. Remember that helmet!

MINSTREL 1: Half-blinded by the dense fog, Siegfried drew his sword. He stepped into the deep ditch he'd just dug. He heard the dragon sweep the ground, seeking him . . . stalking him. Dirt exploded all about him. Rocks crashed like thunder. Then, as if it sensed Siegfried's presence, the dragon came to a dead halt directly above him.

DRAGON: Hold your place, Siegfried. I fear you not!

SIEGFRIED: If it's not me you fear, Beast. Feel you my sword! Take that!

MINSTREL 2: Siegfried thrust his sword up—into the underbelly—once, twice, three times. Then his magic blade cut straight into the dragon's heart.

MINSTREL 1: A torrent of black blood spilled into the ditch. It overflowed and filled the second ditch with wave after wave of thick, boiling blood. Siegfried leaped to one side, free of the rushing torrent.

MINSTREL 2: His mission accomplished, Siegfried withdrew his sword and wiped it clean, but as he did so, a smear of black blood touched his hand.

MINSTREL 1: His hand touched his lips. He could taste the black blood, feel the thick, mucous venom rush through his veins. But then, as birds chirped overhead, magic happened!

MINSTREL 2: With the taste of the blood, Siegfried could understand them . . . their language . . . the language of the very birds that had led him here.

MINSTREL 2: "Treachery," they warned. "Beware of treachery ahead."

NIBELUNG 1: (*Laughter*) So—you've done it! The dragon is dead, is it? Good! Let us go then to the dragon's den. We will share the gold and take the magic ring! (*Slyly*) But first, Siegfried, refresh yourself with this wine.

SIEGFRIED: You have brought wine for me? I think not, Nibelung! That wine bubbles with your treachery! I will drink not your poison, nor will I share the gold!

POET 1: Siegfried grows stronger and wiser with every moment!

POET 2: Record this well. You see, he is about to retrieve the magic gold.

POET 3: How? That twisted creature, the Nibelung, continues to threaten him.

SIEGFRIED: Your poison, Nibelung, I pour, drop by drop, into the dragon's blood. I have cleaned *his* blood from my sword, but now, I shall take *yours*!

NIBELUNG 1: (*Hoarse cackle, but weak*) No . . . no! I am small. I have no weapon!

SIEGFRIED: You are evil . . . treacherous . . . not fit to live! *Go . . . with the dragon*!

SOUNDS A, B: (*Enthusiastic clapping*)

KING: Splendid! Splendid! And does he find the gold?

MINSTREL 1: Indeed, Your Majesty. Siegfried finds the gold and takes it to Worms, where he meets and woos and wins the beautiful Kriemhild.

KING: The gold. What happens to the gold? And the ring?

MINSTREL 2: Ah, some say these treasures rest beneath the waters of the River Rhine—thus we now call that lost treasure the Rhinegold.

KING: Excellent. Excellent! Poets . . . Artists . . . record these events. We are pleased with every word! And now, you are dismissed from our presence. Go in peace with this token of *our* gold for your story. Farewell, most honorable Poets and Minstrels. Farewell!

Myths from Around the World:
Scandinavia

Loki—Evil Tricks in Asgard

INTRODUCTION

Tricksters are scamps, rogues. We see them cavorting in the comics, on television, in films, and maybe even at home. Usually we are ready to laugh at their antics, but not always. Such merry tricksters can show up in literature, too, but the sly tricks of Maria in *Twelfth Night* and Iago in *Othello* bring about dire consequences. No wonder, then, that we view actions of the mythical Loki with a jaundiced eye, for he specializes in chaos.

The stories about Loki are embedded in ancient Nordic lore. Scholars assume these myths were written down in the early thirteenth century by the Icelandic historian, Snorri Sturluson. Various treatises, stories, and poems with their references to Norse mythology make up a collection of these early writings, known today as the Prose Edda.

Like the tales from many cultures, Norse myths include explanations of the origin of the world. In addition, however, they also present a dire prediction of its end. Richard Wagner called this final catastrophe *The Twilight of the Gods,* the last opera of his monumental operatic cycle, *The Ring of the Nibelungs.*

The intricate interfacing of people and gods in Norse mythology, like that in the Greek tales, seems to have become a mosaic for the sagas of world storytelling. Love, sympathy, fear, treachery, compassion, anger, revenge—they're all there, and in the following script, we see Loki the Trickster as the driving force for some of these stories.

Loki is devious, not to be trusted. He breeds evil, literally, yet he can assume a lighthearted manner so ingratiating that Odin, father of the Norse gods, embraces him as a blood brother. Loki often is not what he seems . . . but then, who is?

PRODUCTION NOTES

The natural landscape of Iceland offers such a variety of visual delights that students may easily be tempted to describe them. Certainly, the richness of the Icelandic culture should conjure up any number of pictures. Other artistic stimulations, we hope, will also develop from the production of "Loki—Evil Tricks in Asgard."

The following script calls for approximately seventeen students, a number that can be adjusted by combining the lines of the Giants or Gnomes. One student can handle the sound effects. A minimum of eighteen scripts are required, including one for the teacher.

Trekkers 1 and 2 are the practical, inquisitive human guides for this journey and support the narrative threads. They can be bossy, curious, and helpful . . . like the gods:

Odin, sometimes known as Woden, has come down to us as the namesake for *Wednesday*. He is the father god, with a majestic voice. Thor (we have transformed his name into *Thursday*) is Odin's son—he with the thunderbolt hammer and the firm voice.

The two gods Balder and Tyr (Tyr becomes *Tuesday*) are also sons of Odin. They are courageous, but more timid than some of their god siblings. Fenris, the voracious wolf, is an offspring of Loki. A deeper, growly voice is needed here. Loki the Trickster is the gadfly of all these adventures. He is irrepressible and crafty. His laugh is sly, but he is charismatic. The Gnomes are devious, ancient, and not to be trusted. The script needs good cackles from them. The Giants are big, officious, and blustery, with voices to match.

Sound effects include drumming, jingling of bells, whooshings of air (managed vocally), metallic pounding, sharpening of a metal blade, and maybe the imagined sound of the wolf's jaws closing? Great opportunities for innovations abound! The script, of course, will not truly suffer if these effects are eliminated. The point is to have fun!

Loki—Evil Tricks in Asgard

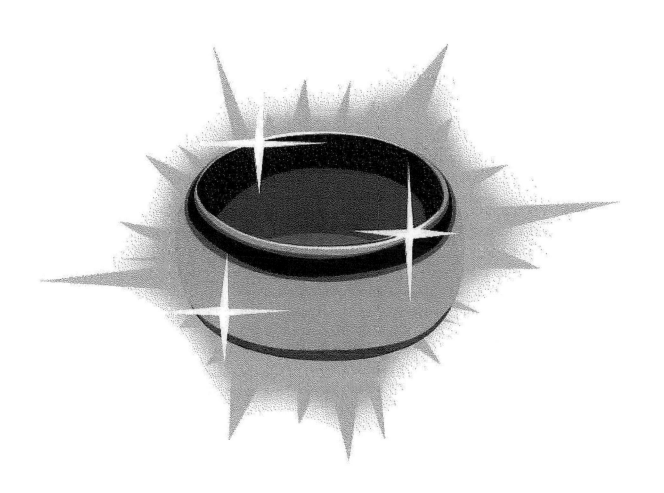

Loki—Evil Tricks in Asgard

Norse Myth

Gnomes 1–4				Sounds A, B			Giants 1–3	
X X X X				X X			X X X	
	Thor			Fenris		Balder, Tyr		
	X			X		X X		
Odin			Trekker 1		Trekker 2		Loki	
X			X		X		X	

TREKKER 1: Where in the world are we? I'm freezing!

TREKKER 2: You said you wanted to go trekking to some faraway, exotic place. Well, this is it! Iceland! What . . . you don't like the crunch of the snow? Step over here—hot springs. Nice, warm water—geysers of it! Iceland has everything!

TREKKER 1: Oh, right . . . and the Arctic Circle is just a hop, skip, and a jump away.

TREKKER 2: Shall I mention Norway? A mere six hundred miles across the water?

TREKKER 1: Now I get it. That's *this* expedition, into a myth from the Norse!

SOUND A: (*Several strong beats on bongo-type drum*)

SOUND B: (*When drumming stops, light jingle of bells during next few speeches*)

TREKKER 2: It's happening! Do you feel it? We're slipping back in time, when people first came to Iceland, when they thought gods and gnomes and giants ruled the universe.

ODIN: Welcome, travelers, to the land that *was*—to our land.

TREKKER 2: (*Hushed*) It's Odin. (*Enthusiastic*) Odin! We *are* back, to maybe three thousand years ago. Bow! Bow to the great god Odin. (*O'-din*)

ODIN: You have come a long way—but you've entered in the wrong way. You've entered the land of the giants.

SOUNDS A, B: (*Whooshing sounds of air/wind*)

TREKKER 1: I see them now. They're huge—and ugly! And the air is freezing!

SOUNDS A, B: (*Another blast of air*)

TREKKER 1: And I'm freezing! Ah, Sir . . . god Odin, those *are* three giants, right?

ODIN: Frost Giants, Traveler. You're in *their* world, far below the gods.

TREKKER 2: Frost Giants? How about *Frost Spirit*? I know some lines about that.

TREKKER 1: At a time like this, with a huge, hairy giant about to breathe icicles down my neck, you're going to recite poetry about him?

TREKKER 2: I am . . . listen! Listen to Whittier: "He comes—he comes—the Frost Spirit comes! From the frozen Labrador, from the icy bridge of the Northern seas, which the white bear wanders o'er, where the fisherman's sail is stiff with ice, and the luckless forms below, in the sunless cold of the lingering night, into marble statues grow. He comes. He comes. The Frost Spirit comes!"

TREKKER 1: Nice. I'd clap, but I'm one of those "luckless forms" freezing into a marble statue! So, John Greenleaf Whittier wrote that, huh? And you're reading it in Iceland . . . today . . . before it was written? Fantastic!

TREKKER 2: Be sensible! (*Whispers*) And be quiet—and look behind you!

GIANT 1: (*Surly, threatening*) You don't belong here. This is *our* world.

GIANT 2: (*Gruffly*) You have entered Jotunheim! (*Jot'-un-hime*)

ODIN: Oh, Jotunheim is just one of our nine worlds. We'll welcome you in Asgard, though. It's my world, the world of the gods. (*Az'-guard*)

GIANT 3: (*Threatening laugh*) Not welcome for long, Odin. Not for long!

GIANT 1: If you do go to Asgard, look for one like us up there—Loki. If you find him, we warn you . . . *watch out!* (*Low'-kee*)

SOUNDS A, B: (*Several blasts of air; air fades away*)

TREKKER 1: Loki? He's here in Asgard? Is he a frost giant, or is he another god?

LOKI: (*Laughs*) I am neither—and both. Confused? Of course. Today you are strangers in a strange land. Nothing will be what it *seems* to be.

ODIN: Loki . . . that's enough! (*Pause*) So, Travelers, now you have met Loki, my blood brother.

TREKKER 2: He's your blood brother? Do you mean that, seriously?

ODIN: Show them, Loki. Show them the scar.

LOKI: Oh, it was eons ago, but like yesterday. I remember . . . and I know Odin remembers. We both bear the scars. You tell them.

ODIN: You see, I heard Loki laughing in the world below, so I called him up from Jotunheim. We agreed on many things and could laugh about many things. Finally, I suggested we seal our friendship—with blood.

LOKI: Of course, I was honored—the great god Odin. Without hesitation, I seized my long dagger. (*Slowly*) I tested the blade—the deadly point—and I pricked my skin. Blood rose to the surface.

ODIN: Go on, Loki!

LOKI: (*Slowly, intently*) The blade seemed to move by itself. Breathless and numb, I watched a long, wet, red streak creep down my arm.

ODIN: "Now, mine," I told him.

LOKI: I pricked his skin, then drew the blade across his veins.

ODIN: "Deeper!" I told him.

LOKI: I heard him. I dug it in deep. His blood strained to escape. I stared as something thick and red and squirming slowly snaked its way out.

TREKKER 2: Then what?

ODIN: I told him, "Well, done, brother Loki! Well done!"

LOKI: God Odin clasped his arm against mine. His blood entered my body, and mine entered his. We were blood brothers now. Already I could feel the power of Odin course through my veins.

GNOME 1: (*Scornful cackle*) His *protection*, you mean! Blood brothers—ha! Always Loki's tricks, his thefts—yet he always goes free! Ask Thor!

TREKKER 1: (*Loud whisper*) Sh. Don't look now, but that's a little gnome!

TREKKER 2: (*Whispers*) Loki's gone. We're moving on. It's yet *another* world!

GNOME 2: Just ask the god Thor; he'll tell you about Loki.

ODIN: Indeed, he knows Loki well. Thor, you see, is one of my sons and the strongest of them all. He is wedded to a lovely goddess, Sif.

THOR: She *is* beautiful. When I saw her long, golden hair, I knew she had to be mine. And we were happy, until one night, Loki sneaked into our room and stole every shining strand, every golden lock of Sif's hair!

TREKKER 2: You were there? Loki must have made himself invisible.

THOR: And silent, too!

GNOME 1: (*Snarly cackle*) But *you* weren't! You were furious! Even in our world, Darkalfheim, we heard you. I still hear you! (*Dar'-kalf-highm*)

THOR: So I shouted to him, "Loki! I know it's you! What in the name of the gods has happened here? Every single golden strand of Sif's hair is gone! She's bald!"

GNOME 1: Then Loki laughed at you.

THOR: He did, but that didn't stop me! I asked him, "Do you think you can get away with this? *You* would do such a deed? *You*, blood brother to my father?" Of course, at that he tried to squirm out of his evil trick.

LOKI: Thor, I'm sorry, really I am. I'll make it up to you.

THOR: I didn't believe him, but I asked, "How *can* you restore her hair?"

LOKI: Not restore it, Thor, make it *better*. Look, I will go to the gnomes. They will spin threads of glorious gold, finer than her hair before.

GNOME 2: That's when he came to us, to make the golden hair and save him.

SOUNDS A, B: (*Intermittent rhythmic sounds of hammer on metal during next lines*)

LOKI: I much admire your work, though I like not visiting this underground cave. Yet with all your skill, and your gold, and your bronze, I know you will make Thor happy, even his vain wife, Sif.

GNOME 2: We do your bidding, Loki. We will make amends for you—again.

LOKI: Yes—and while you're at it, hammer out another gift or two for Thor and my Aesir friends who live in Asgard. (*A'-sir*)

GNOME 1: He was arrogant, as usual, but the work went well.

SOUND A: (*Metal clangs against metal.*)

GNOME 1: First, we fashioned a magic ring, then a sword that would be forever sharp, and then a flying boat, so big it could carry all the gods *and* their horses, yet fold up and fit in the palm of your hand.

TREKKER 1: I am very impressed. Very!

GNOME 2: Last, my brother fashioned hair out of pure gold for Thor's wife. It was an artistic triumph. It actually grew on her head! Loki praised us.

LOKI: A magical design! Inventive—hair more beautiful than the original. Surely you must be the cleverest goldsmith in this world.

GNOME 1: I don't think so, Loki. Our brother is far better. *He* is the Master. His art and his craft are superior to all the workmen in this mountain.

LOKI: (*Laughs*) Who says so? I challenge you to prove that!

GNOME 1: Done! And what if our brother wins this wager? What then?

LOKI: It will never happen! Indeed, I am so sure of that, I'll offer you a prize—my head. If your brother wins, you can cut off my head.

GNOME 3: Perfect! As Master Goldsmith, I accept your challenge. However, my apprentice must work the bellows. The fire must burn hot and steady.

ODIN: I was not present, but they told me. When the Master gnome began his work, they were instantly in trouble. The apprentice who plied the bellows for the fire began dancing around and crying out in pain.

GNOME 4: Master! Get that fly away from me. He's biting me on the cheek! I cannot work the bellows! The fire flickers! *Ouch! Stop it!*

ODIN: The little gnome tried desperately to drive the fly away, even to kill it. But no matter how hard he tried, the fly continued to pinch and bite him. Was it Loki? Maybe. Still, the Master poured more and more gold on the fire, crafting one beautiful piece of work after the other.

GNOME 4: Oh, Master—a wild boar with golden bristles, and a magic gold ring!

ODIN: Finally, the Master Goldsmith poured a lump of iron into the fire.

GNOME 4: Oh, no! Please, stop! Master! Make it stop! Something's biting me! I'm bleeding! *Ouch!* (*Whimpers*) I'm bleeding! I can't see!

SOUND A: (*A crash of metal*)

GNOME 3: Now look what you've done—the fire's out! The iron is ruined—the magic hammer! The handle is too short! It's ruined!

ODIN: But no. When Loki presented the magic gifts to the gods, everyone knew that it was the gift to Thor, that miraculous hammer, Miolnir, that had won the day for the Master Goldsmith. (*Miohl'-neer*)

TREKKER 2: Hold on! I think I remember lines about Thor.

TREKKER 1: Right. Fantasy time-out for poetry. Make it brief, huh?

TREKKER 2: It's The Challenge of Thor. Chime in when you're ready. Be Thor!

TREKKER 1: Okay! "I am the God Thor, I am the War God, I am the Thunderer!"

TREKKER 2: You've got it! "Here in my Northland, my fastness and fortress, reign I forever! Here, amid icebergs, rule I the nations; this is my hammer, Miolner the mighty; giants and sorcerers cannot withstand it!"

TREKKER 1: Yeah! "Mine eyes are the lightning; the wheels of my chariot roll in the thunder, the blows of my hammer ring in the earthquake!"

TREKKER 2: Henry Wadsworth Longfellow. Boy, if that poet could see us now!

TREKKER 1: Or maybe help out that trickster Loki. Oh, oh! The gnome is moving in. I think Loki's about to lose his head. Wasn't that the wager?

ODIN: It was. You might think Loki was cornered, but listen to this.

GNOME 1: We're ready for you, Loki. You owe us your head. You lost the bet.

LOKI: (*Oily*) Oh, to be sure, I owe you my head. Please, do take it.

SOUND B: (*Sharpening sound*)

GNOME 2: A sharp knife, Loki. Just one stroke, and your head is ours.

LOKI: Exactly so, but with one consideration: you must not mar, touch, or scratch my *neck*. My *neck* was not in the wager. Correct? (*Laughs*)

GNOMES 1, 2, 3: Loki!

GNOME 1: Then sew his lips together! We never want to hear him speak again!

LOKI: Now, hold on, friends. (*Muffled speech*) This was only a joke!

GNOMES 1, 2, 3: You lose. We win. Good-bye, god Loki! (*Strong laughter fades away.*)

TREKKER 1: Wow! That's horrible! How does Loki manage to eat all sewn up?

ODIN: His wife's sharp knife cut the threads. You know, she was an ogress.

TREKKER 1: He was married to a female ogre? Oh, great. Did they have children?

ODIN: Yes, as a matter of fact, three monsters—the worst, a ravenous, ferocious wolf, Fenris.

TREKKER 2: And therein lies a tale?

ODIN: It is difficult to speak fairly about Fenris. My son Tyr was his victim.

TREKKER 1: Victim of a wolf! Oh, no! What happened?

LOKI: (*Laughs*) Can you imagine? He brought my Fenris up to Asgard!

ODIN: Loki, I had to. Fenris was growing bigger and bigger every day, eating everything in sight. He was a threat to everyone. Bringing him into Asgard, I hoped to calm him . . . gentle him, pet him.

TREKKER 1: I don't think this worked.

LOKI: Of course not! You should have heard the arguments, seen the ropes and chains, heard the two gods, Tyr and his brother Balder, plotting.

BALDER: Tyr, the gods are frightened of this beast. It grows more fierce every day. Some gods in the council actually wish to kill him.

TYR: No! They can't be serious. Asgard is devoted to peace and protection. To slay Fenris is against everything we stand for.

BALDER: But something must be done. You, Tyr, you're the *only one* who will even go near the beast now.

TYR: Yes, and he grows hungry. He must be fed, Balder. I am not afraid.

BALDER: But others are! Tyr, listen. The council has decided that Fenris must be tied up, bound with rope so strong he can never get free.

LOKI: (*Laughs*) How those gods could dream! My friends, nothing worked! Fenris could not be tamed. He could not be bound!

BALDER: Perhaps he will not be able to break an *iron* chain, Tyr.

TYR: We tried that. He snapped it apart.

BALDER: Something stronger, then, something that can't be broken. But what?

TYR: Who could make such a thing? (*Pause*) Wait! I know—those gnomes!

SOUND A: (*Brief pounding of metal against metal*)

GNOME 3: (*Cackles*) It was only a matter of time, eh? Is it the magic you need?

TYR: Your magic, Master—your craftsmanship, your artistry—

BALDER: We need something very special, something to hold Fenris tight.

GNOME 3: Aha. I see. You will need the silken rope, one that will never break.

TREKKER 1: A silken rope? How is that supposed to hold a wild, ferocious beast?

TREKKER 2: Hush. Loki warned us: "Nothing will be what it *seems* to be."

GNOME 3: (*Whispers*) We begin. We begin: first, the sound of a cat's footsteps—

GNOME 1: (*Whispers*) Hairs from a woman's beard, the roots of a mountain—

GNOME 2: (*Whispers*) Longings of the bear, voices of fishes, and spittle of birds.

GNOME 3: Done! Take it, ye gods, and remind Odin who created this silken rope.

LOKI: I saw that rope. It was a masterpiece. I was afraid for Fenris. He was strong and violent, but he was not stupid. I stood, watching the gods.

FENRIS: (*Low growl*) So, Tyr, you've come again, I see—dragged me out to this god-forsaken island like a bag of bones and a pile of putrid dirt.

TYR: Sorry, Fenris, but see, this is all about *your* strength. We're hoping you can test this silken rope for us. It's *supposed* to be invincible.

BALDER: (*Whispers*) Tyr, this will never work! He will snap it in two!

TYR: (*Whispers*) No! The gnomes worked the magic arts. If Fenris tries to break the rope, it will only grow stronger. It will never, ever break. (*Coaxing*) Well, Fenris, let's see how this works. First, I put the rope about you, like this. See how slight it is? You're so strong, it *can't possibly* hold you. The rope is bound to break. It's nothing but silk.

FENRIS: Silk? (*Growls*) I don't believe it. Prove it! Put your hand in my mouth and leave it there until I snap this so-called *silken* rope.

BALDER: Oh, Tyr, no, you can't do that! Fenris . . . .

146

TYR: It's all right, Balder. I'll . . . I'll do it. (*Pause*) All right, Fenris, open your mouth. Here's my hand, my right hand.

FENRIS: (*Louder growling*) I'm warning you!

TYR: (*Hiss*) Balder, the rope! Pull it tight! Perfect! He'll never get loose!

FENRIS: (*Several really deep, loud growls*)

SOUND B: (*Slow, squeaking sound of jaws closing*)

TYR: No! Stop, Fenris! No! Balder! My hand—it's gone! Gone!

TREKKER 1: Whew! Snap your fingers, man! We have to leave this place!

TREKKER 2: Uh-oh! Things *may* be what they seem. Let's see *your* right hand!

TREKKER 1: (*Brief, brief pause, then . . .*) *Oh, no!* Let's get out of here!

Select Bibliography

The listings below represent the major writings consulted for this book. Eight main reference books proved invaluable in the research for each myth and its cultural and historical background. Web sites were frequently helpful. Sites on these pages were all accessed in 2008.

MAIN REFERENCE BOOKS

Campbell, Joseph. *Hero with a Thousand Faces.* New York: World, 1971.

Campbell, Joseph, with Bill Moyers. *The Power of Myth.* New York: Anchor, 1991.

Durant, Will. *The Age of Faith,* Part IV of *The Story of Civilization.* New York: Simon & Schuster, 1950.

———. *The Life of Greece,* Part II of *The Story of Civilization.* New York: Simon & Schuster, 1939.

———. *Our Oriental Heritage,* Part I of *The Story of Civilization.* New York: Simon & Schuster, 1954.

Highet, Gilbert. *The Classical Tradition.* Oxford: University of Oxford Press, 1967.

Medieval Folklore. Edited by Carl Lindahl, John McNamara, and John Lindow. Oxford: Oxford University Press, 2002.

The New Larousse Encyclopedia of Mythology. London: Hamlyn, 1968.

The Oxford Classical Dictionary. Edited by N. G. L. Hammond and H. H. Scullard. Oxford: Clarendon Press, 1970.

Oxford Companion to Classical Literature. Edited by Sir Paul Harvey. Oxford: University of Oxford Press, 1969.

World Mythology. Edited by Roy Willis. London: Baird, 2006.

ADDITIONAL BOOKS FOR INDIVIDUAL MYTHS

Africa

Belcher, Stephen. *African Myths of Origin.* London: Penguin, 2005.

Pelton, Robert. *The Trickster in West Africa.* Berkeley: University of California Press, 1989.

Scheub, Harold. *A Dictionary of African Myths.* New York: Oxford University Press, 2000.

Selected Books for Children

Cole, Joanna. *Best-loved Folktales of the World.* Garden City, NY: Doubleday, 1982.

Giddens, Sandra, and Owen Giddens. *African Mythology.* New York: Rosen, 2006.

Mbugua, Kioi. *Inkishu, Myths and Legends of the Maasai.* Nairobi, Kenya: Jacaranda, 1994.

Olivier, John J. *The Wisdom of African Mythology.* Largo, FL: Top of the Mountain, 1994.

Parrinder, Goeffrey. *African Mythology.* New York: Bedrick, 1986.

Web Sites

www.gutenberg.org/files 22282/22282-h22282-h.htm (Uncle Remus)

www.uiowa.edu/~africart/toc/people/yoruba.html (information on Yoruba)

en.wikipedia.org/wiki/Cocoa (cocoa)

en.wikipedia.org/wiki/African_mythology (African traditional religion)

en.wikipedia.org/wiki/African_deities (deities, especially Eshu)

American Indian

Bierhorst, John. *The Mythology of North America.* New York: William Morrow, 1985.

Bruchac, Joseph. *North American Stories.* Golden, CO: Fulcrum, 1991.

Burland, Cottie. *North American Indian Mythology.* Revised by Marion Wood. New York: Bedrick/Hamlyn, 1987.

Gill, John Kaye. *Dictionary of the Chinook Jargon with Examples of Its Use.* Portland, OR: J.K. Gill, 1884.

Journals of Lewis and Clark. Abridged ed., 1 vol. Edited by Bernard De Voto Boston: Houghton Mifflin, 1953.

Lummis, Charles F. *Pueblo Indian Folk-Stories.* Lincoln: University of Nebraska Press, 1992. (Previously published, New York: Century, 1910; originally published 1894.).

Ruby, Robert H., and John A. Brown. *The Chinook Indians.* Norman, OK, and London: University of Oklahoma Press, 1976.

Spence, Lewis. *Myths of the North American Indians.* New York: Gramercy, 1994. (Originally published, London: n.p., 1914).

Selected Books for Children

Martin, Rafe, and David Shannon. *The Boy Who Lived with the Seals.* New York: Putnam, 1993.

Ross, Pamela. *The Chinook People.* Mankato, MN: Bridgestone/Capstone Press, 1999.

Web Sites

en.wikipedia.org/wiki/Lewis_Spence

wikipedia.org/wiki/Chinookan

chinookindian.com/greene/chinook_FAQ-ans-08.htm

enwikipedia.org/wiki/Chinooks

www.chinooknation.org

enwikipedia.org/wiki/John-Jacob-Astor

wikipedia.org/wiki/Fur-Trade

Arabia

"Assyro-Babylonian Mythology." In *The New Larousse Encyclopedia of Mythology*. London: Hamlyn, 1968.

Graves, Robert. *The Greek Myths*. Vols.1 and 2. Baltimore, MD: Penguin, 1957.

Heidel, Alexander. *The Gilgamesh Epic and Old Testament Parallels*. Chicago: University of Chicago Press, 1949.

Mason, Herbert. *Gilgamesh*. New York: New American Library, 1972.

Sanders, N. K. *The Epic of Gilgamesh*. Rev. ed. Harmondsworth, UK: Penguin, 1964.

Selected Books for Children

Finkel, Irving. *The Hero King Gilgamesh*. Lincolnwood, IL: NTC Publishing Group, 1998. (First published, London: British Museum Press, 1998.)

Web Sites

en.wikipedia.org/wikiGilgamesh.

en.wikipedia.org/wiki/Epic_of_Gilgamesh

www.macedonia.org.uk/events/finkel.htm.

www.wsu.edu/~dee/MESO/GILG.HTM.

Greece

Chabon, Michael. "Secret Skin." *The New Yorker,* March 10, 2008, 64–69.

Dante, Alighieri. "Canto VI." In *The Inferno*. Translated by John Ciardi. New York: New American Library, 1982.

Graves, Robert. *The Greek Myths*. Vols.1 and 2. Baltimore, MD: Penguin, 1957.

Vergil. "Book 6." In *The Aeneid*. Translated by Frank O. Copley. Indianapolis, IN: Bobbs-Merrill, 1965.

India

Ions, Veronica. *Indian Mythology*. London: Hamlyn, 1967.

Kirk, James A. *Stories of the Hindus*. New York: Macmillan, 1972.

Selected Books for Children

Husain, Shahrukh. *Demons, Gods & Holy Men from Indian Myths and Legends*. World Mythology series. New York: Bedrick, 1987.

Jaffrey, Madhur. *Seasons of Splendour*. New York: Atheneum, 1985.

Kerven, Rosalind. *The Slaying of the Dragon*. London: Deutsch, 1987.

Web Sites

en.wikipedia.org/wiki/Vishnu

www.sacred-texts.com/hin/dutt/rama01.htm.

en.wikipedia.org/wiki/Ramayana

Ireland

Blue Guide, Ireland. Edited by Ian Robertson. London: Benn & Rand McNally, 1979.

Cuchulain of Muirthemne: The Story of the Men of the Red Branch of Ulster Arranged and Put into English by Lady Gregory with a Preface by W.B.Yeats. London: John Murray, 1902.

Hogain, Daithi. *Myth, Legend and Romance.* New York: Prentice Hall,1991.

"The Ulster Cycle." In *Ancient Irish Tales,* edited by Tom Peete Cross and Clark Harris Slover. New York: Holt, 1936.

Web Sites

www.gutenberg.org/files/25502/25502-h/25502-h.htm (e-book of *Hero-Myths and Legends of the British Race* by Maud I. Ebbutt)

en.wikipedia.org/wiki/Cuchulain

en.wikipedia.org/wiki/Ulster_Cycle

en.wikipedia.org/wiki/Celtic_Mythology

Scandinavia

Guerber, H. A. *Myths of the Norsemen.* New York: Dover, 1992. (Originally published in 1909.)

Sagas and Myths of the Northmen. Translated by Jesse Byock. Suffolk, UK: Penguin, 2006.

Poetry

"Balder Dead." In *Poetical Works of Matthew Arnold,* edited by C. B. Tinker and H. F. Lowry. London: Oxford, 1961. (Poem first published in 1855.)

"The Challenge of Thor" from "The Saga of King Olaf" in "Tales of a Wayside Inn." In *Poems and Other Writings of Henry Wadsworth Longfellow,* edited by J. D. McClatchy. New York: Penguin Putnam, 2000.

Whittier, John Greenleaf. "The Frost Spirit." In *Complete Poetical Works of John Greenleaf Whittier.* Cambridge: Riverside/Houghton, Mifflin, 1902. (Originally published in 1899.)

Selected Books for Children

Climo, Shirley. *Stolen Thunder.* New York: Clarion, 1994.

Colum, Padraic. *Children of Odin.* New York: Macmillan, 1984. (Originally published in 1920.)

———. *A Treasury of Irish Folklore.* New York: Kilkenny/Crown, 1989.

D'Aulaire, Ingri, and Edgar Parin. *D'Aulaires' Book of Norse Myths.* New York: New York Review of Books, 2005. (Originally published in 1967.)

Green, Jen. *Gods and Goddesses in the Daily Life of the Vikings.* Columbus, OH: Bedrick/ McGraw-Hill, 2003. (Originally produced by Salariya in Brighton.)

The Macmillan Atlas of Irish History. Edited by Sean Duffy. New York: Macmillan, 1997.

Philip, Neil. *Odin's Family.* New York: Orchard, 1996.

Spence, Lewis. *Germany.* Myths and Legends Series. London: Studio Editions, 1993. (Originally published, n.p.: Harrap & Co., n.d.)

Web Sites

en.wikipedia.org/wiki/Prose_Edda

en.wikipedia.org/wiki/List_of_Norse_gods

en.wikipedia.org/wiki/Ragnar%C%B6k

en.wikipedia.org/wiki/Loki

en.wikipedia.org/wiki/Mjolnir

en.wikipedia.org/wiki/Iceland

About the Author

Photo by Calabash.

Ann N. Black is a native of Iowa and a graduate of Northwestern University, where she received a B.S. from the School of Communication, then worked as an actress and a writer and producer of children's radio dramas. Married to a theatre professor, she, too, switched to the academic life. Her experiences as a critic judge, from directing, teaching, and writing led her to a M.A. in English and Oral Interpretation from the University of North Texas, then to an assistant professorship of literature and creative writing at Northwestern State University of Louisiana. As an enthusiastic member of Society of Children's Book Writers and Illustrators, she continues to write for young people. *Born Storytellers: Readers Theatre Celebrates the Lives and Literature of Classic Authors* is her recent companion book of scripts for high school students.